T0159053

choices . . .

A UNIVERSAL GUIDE
FOR RATIONAL THINKING

KYLA NELSEN

BALBOA.
PRESS

A DIVISION OF HAY HOUSE

Balboa Press books may be ordered through booksellers or by contacting:

Balboa Press
A Division of Hay House
1663 Liberty Drive
Bloomington, IN 47403
www.balboapress.com
1 (877) 407-4847

Because of the dynamic nature of the Internet, any web addresses or links contained in this book may have changed since publication and may no longer be valid. The views expressed in this work are solely those of the author and do not necessarily reflect the views of the publisher, and the publisher hereby disclaims any responsibility for them.

The author of this book does not dispense medical advice or prescribe the use of any technique as a form of treatment for physical, emotional, or medical problems without the advice of a physician, either directly or indirectly. The intent of the author is only to offer information of a general nature to help you in your quest for emotional and spiritual well-being. In the event you use any of the information in this book for yourself, which is your constitutional right, the author and the publisher assume no responsibility for your actions.

Any people depicted in stock imagery provided by Thinkstock are models, and such images are being used for illustrative purposes only. Certain stock imagery © Thinkstock.

Print information available on the last page.

ISBN: 978-1-5043-7390-6 (sc)
ISBN: 978-1-5043-7391-3 (e)

Balboa Press rev. date: 05/08/2017

rational thinking

+

common sense and decency

+

love and compassion

=

world peace

contents

dedication

This book is dedicated to my very special Mom. This book is the result of her patient, loving support and she inspires me daily! To be loving and kind, even when that person may not be what she wants for them, not exactly what she had in mind …. and yet, she is supportive, anyway!

It is also dedicated to my Children … who continue to inspire me, on a daily basis! I consider them as my "walking reward" …. for all of my energy, effort, and love …. plus time, and their lives and how they have maneuvered life …I am very blessed … and extremely proud!

As time goes on, life gets better and better. And, as I believe that, so it is! I truly thank my Mother and Children, for living through the hard knocks of my past, with me. And, along with my Son's beautiful wife, (in so many ways), …. and my wonderful Grandchildren …..we, together, grow stronger and better … as awesome individuals, and as a very loving, special Family, that I love very much … this book is for you …

After the "irrational" election, in the United States . . . .

And the Discontentment felt by ALL . . . .

Around the World . . . . . .

This Guide is for ALL, to educate and relate the concept of "Rational Thinking", and the fact that we make Choices . . . .

The "Power of Choice" is common to ALL . . . . if we educate ourselves and each other, with the understanding of rational thinking . . . .then, move FORWARD, with "new" knowledge and a broader concept as to what LIFE is about?

CHOICE is demonstrated by all . . . . it is what we do with our "choice", that really matters . . . .

RATIONAL THINKING changes ALL . . . .

every moment . . .

we make choices . . . .

take control ....

of

your ......

C   H   O   I   C   E   S

...make them   P O S I T I V E ...

This is meant to be a guide . . . .
for any person . . . .

on this earth . . . . . .

to learn a way to . . . . .
process your thoughts . . . . .

in a rational way . . . .

evolving into a universe . . . .

of caring individuals . . . .

making "rational" choices .. . . .

Sometimes letting go . . . . . .

moves you . . . . .

towards . . . .

something . . . . . .

N E W . . . .

always ....

figure out .....

what you are ....

R E A L L Y needing ....

there are ....

many D I S G U I S E S ......

"I will ....?"

or

"I won't ...... ?"

what is.....?

your theme ....?

is your cup ....

half full ....?

or ....

half empty........?

blaming others ....

for the way ....

you are ....

won't help ....

your choices ....

**rational thinking
with conscientious thought
process**

+

practice

=

**a more rational international
community**

be . . . .

special . . . . .

are you a person?

what color is your blood?

then,

we are the same . . . . .

what is ....

L O V E ....?

why ....?

if we all ....

make the choice ....

to be **H A P P Y** ....

concentrate ....

on that ....

sever the past!!!! ....

and, move forward ....

foreword

This book is intended to CHANGE the World, as we know it now!

With a message to provide a common theme of thought,
    which applies to all of humanity . . . . .
        it provides simple, yet effective, ways ; ; ; ;

    to change your thought processes . . . .

        therefore, changing your life!!!

With enlightening and enhancing ways to change our thinking . . . .

    we can start coming together again, one by one . . . .

    towards the common good of ALL!!!

With a calm and comforting message that will start overcoming all of
the chaos . . . throughout the World . . . .

garbage In . . . .

garbage out . . . .

good thoughts In . . . .

good results and positive life . . .

bad thoughts in . . . .

chaos . . . negative . . . confusion . . .

discontentment . . . . selfishness . . . .
etc., etc. . .

stop!

do you like ....????

your life...............???

letter from the author :

It is my hope that this simple Guide, designed to re-educate and teach the rational ways of thinking and perceiving life, will enhance a very enlightened reader, who decides to pick up this book. It was never a strength of mine, being able to read and comprehend what an author was saying to me. In this book, I intend to relate to you, as if you were me . . . . sure that I want the best possible life for myself, just looking for special ways to live that life. Not an easy "assignment", given the diversity of the monetary systems, where the rich get richer and the poor get poorer. It is the driving force for writing this book, to point out that we all have the privilege of "choice". And, if . . . at the end of the day, we do not like our lives as they are, we can look at the choices we have made along the way.

A Guide, combining common sense and rational thinking, along with intuition and listening to our inner voice, (and then monitoring what that voice is saying) . . . along with love . . . and SEVERING OUR PAST . . . to start a "new" way to think and interact with each other.

From the White House of the United States of America, to prisons, to schools, to Churches, to libraries, to any and all bookstores around the World, this will become a Universal Guide to begin NEW thoughts of PEACE . . . . .

one choice ....

at a time ....

not perfect ....

Just always better ....

concentrate ....

on your choices ....

"if I can do it ...."

"anyone can ...."

* * * * * * * * * * * * * *

it is the process ....

not the result ....

after the result ....

you have the process ....

to the next result ....

each of us ....

has ....

something to offer ....

figure it out ....

or not? ....

your choice! ....

we can all ....

get along ....

if we each ....

make that ....

C H O I C E .....

do not ....

OVERTHINK ....

* * * * * * * * * * * * * * *

"kiss theory" ....

K EE P ....

it ....

simple ....

STUPID ....

rational thinking

The "process" of Rational Thinking is the knowledge of the power within our minds. To evolve from being an "emotional thinker", to a "rational thinker", could be the difference for a potential gunman, between causing harm by pulling a trigger ... OR NOT! No violence is "rational" ... if you go slowly backwards in the evolution of a gunman, for example, or a rapist, etc., you will see an injured child along the way ... choices were not a concept in their life, only being a victim of pain or some form of negativity. Before that, you would see an innocent baby, clinging to it's mother, like every child born.

We all bleed the same blood, if you live on this planet and are a human being ... we are the same ...

Being together as humans, helping each other, is what a world of "rational thinkers" would do, and instead? We have a world with extreme negativity in parts of it, almost feeding off of itself. We have a world of people who need a lot of help, and a world of people with resources. "CHOICES" ... rational or irrational ... each person on this planet has choices, whether realized or not. This Guide will educate all to their potential, and therefore, POWER.

RATIONAL THINKING

A thought . . .

(then, pause yourself . . . as if the "Director" of your own "movie")

Imagine . . .

yourself standing up and away from yourself, as if you can watch yourself being the star of your own movie....

Think Through . . .

your own thought, and ask yourself some of the following questions:

1. Is my "emotion" involved in this thought?
   (rational thoughts do not include emotions . . . only facts and "what is real" . . .

2. Does my thought Make Sense?
   - Is it right or wrong?
   - Good or bad?
   - Positive or negative?
   - Will it hurt anyone?

3. What will the overall results of my thought be?
   - Forward motion?
   - Destruction?

4. Any other options?

RATIONAL THINKING

After you have the knowledge that so much is possible...that thoughts create our choices...that our choices, over time ...create our life....after you gain and grasp the concept of "choice", and "rational thinking", it is only a matter of time, that you will begin to discover a pattern for yourself.

We all start this life in the same way, the miracle called "life". This book does not address life "style", such as religion, politics, race, etc. It only addresses the fact that we are all human beings, born with purpose to give to this World. Somewhere along the way, the negative, "ways of separation", kind of thinking got started. This book is designed to reverse the momentum of negativity . . . before energy with so much negativity is created to destroy us all!

This is an attempt at a "wake up call" ...to the tone of a new administration in the White House. This is a Guide for ALL ... to start a "new normal" for the World!

Most of this book was written twenty years ago. This chapter, and the concept of rational thinking, was unknown to me at that time. "Had I only known" ...my life would have had a much different direction.

"You don't know what you don't know" ... right? I lived along, "normal", not knowing that I had "choices" of what I allowed into my life. And "choices" about how I reacted to other people's input. I used to talk to all of my "people" ... take a vote ... go by majority rule ... to live MY life ... what?

After over two years of ongoing classes and therapy involving rational thinking, I learned that my life was my own to decide. I had to please myself with the choices I made, no one else, a concept that I struggle with, to this day.

Rational Thinking is not something that you learn and "just know". It is a "concept" and a "process" ... almost a way of life to "decide" that, "you are at the controls now" ... (of your own life and how you react to others.)

you don't know . . . .

what you . . . .

Don't know . . . .

time goes fast ....

when you are spending time ....

Being authentic ....

Time goes very slowly ....

When you are not ....

being authentic!!! ....

if you spend your time ....

improving your own ....

C H O I C E S ....

rather than criticizing others ....

both will be better ....

what does ....

your inner voice ....

tell you ??? ....

do you have the control ....

of your choices ??? ....

or is life ....

choosing for you ??????? ....

if life ....

is choosing ....

for you ....

take back the control ....

of your own ....

C H O I C E S...............

the time is ....

N O W ....

to make the choice ....

to change any ....

N E G A T I V E ...

the more **P O S I T I V E** ....

the less **N E G A T I V E** ....

you can do it ....

if you want to ....

D E C I D E

to make ....

positive choices ....

who ....

are ....

you???? ....

it will be good ....

when I can say ....

I did it!!! ....

my life ....

is ....

my choice ....

my life is ....

my "choices" ....

rational thinking and choices

Over time, if we each learned to sever the past (except for special, good, positive memories) . . . (and learning from our mistakes) . . . if we would each take responsibility for going inside of our own minds, day by day, moment by moment . . . and become "our own best friend". If we could take these concepts and start teaching our children how to think in a rational way. If we could stop hating each other for the differences, and come together, as human beings .... all "IN THIS TOGETHER"!

Rational thought would not process harming another (except in self-defense) ... in most instances, it would involve emotion or insanity. Rational thinking would have a person stop first ... "does it make sense"? "would it harm another"? "what would the consequences be"? If rationality became a "thread" to weave and mend the World, it would be a blessing for us all!

As a Mother, Grandmother, Daughter, Friend ... it only makes sense for all of us on this Earth to start getting along!

choices

I will be writing some versions of this book for our Children, and our Teenagers. It is my hope that as this concept spreads, to replace all of the negativity building up in this World, it will become a refreshing, new way to think. It is a way to stop and do a self-analysis ... to ask some important questions ...

1. Do I like what I see? Why?

2. What can I do better? How?

3. What can I not control, that I have been trying to control?

4. What changes do I want to make? How?

youcannotgoback...

we all ....

make mistakes ....

just don't ....

make it ....

a theme ....

stand back ....

and,

look at ....

your life ....

the united states election

The United States of America, as a collective, made an extremely important "choice", in our last election cycle. It is a perfect example of the "power" of "choice" … it is what happens when choices, involving others, evolve into something that some do not want! It is called "Democracy". The level of "television drama" involved in this election cycle, is very comparable. It has become a "show" for some … there is a huge divide, and it, personally … scares me, that the "United States" has become so divided. Also called "Democracy".

The outcome of this election was a surprise to many. As this is written, is there any way we can foresee the results of our "Choice"? What will happen? One thing being for sure … and another "new" reason to push towards the "trend" of this book …that there is the HUGE need to find a reason to come together as "One" again … the "United" States of America.

With the "method" of rational thinking … with the knowledge … the desire for a better society … for a better World … "Rational Thinking", by each individual, can play a huge part in getting PAST what we, "The United States of America", as a Nation, just experienced. Then, moving forward … if we can only LEARN from what happened?

If we can all realize that not only The United States of America, but the entire World, is involved. If we can stop … learn … listen … sever the past … begin a new way … practice a NEW way to think … to eliminate all of the negative, irrational ways … it would become a better life for ALL of us …

When we begin to heal from all of the negativity forced upon us, and when we learn that we have power over each and every choice we make, it is very empowering. Not that we have the choice over all that happens ... some things are beyond our control. We do have control over how we react, though ... that is where we can involve rational thinking.

As each of us become aware of Rational Thinking, and start practicing with our choices, it will be amazing the differences ... it would change everything ... it changed my life! I had been the "victim", creating a situation with my thinking. Overall, it has taken years of "process" and "practice", to learn and change. Then, constant monitoring, to shape and evolve into the person with the life that, hopefully, matches my purpose in this life ... not just a waste of time, (which is also a choice) your life ...

your choice ...

your creation ...

your thoughts ...

your results ...

introduction

How can I write a book that will make you want to pick it up and read it? And, how can I write a book that will add something to your life? I want to make a difference! What do I have to offer?

The main thing that I can offer is inspiration that you can "be" whoever you WANT to be! We all have so much power within our minds ... it all involves "choice", and until we realize that every second of every day involves choice, we give our power away. I am guilty, like so many people, of allowing so many influences to take over my power. My husband, my children, my Mother, some "friends". Sometimes, I listen to them. Then my choices become theirs. I had this concept floating in my mind for over ten years, and knew that I would learn more about the concept of "choices" as I wrote. Just as I hope that you can learn as you read. My goal is not to change your life by what I say... only to enhance it. If I can give just one person the inspiration to change just one thing in their life, by what I say, I will have succeeded!

"Choice" ... the definition in Webster's Dictionary is ...

"Power, right or liberty to choose ..."

"Carefully selected ..."

Now tell me, that those are not powerful words. People end up in marriages they do not like, or end up having babies they are not ready for ... and, then wonder why? Each and every person on this Earth has no "choice" to begin with, right? None of us have any say about it.

Then, due to our individual circumstances, we end up as different as we all are. … from a homeless person to Bill Gates, the richest person in the World! But why?

The concept of Choice, that is where I believe the answer lies. People can blame every circumstance in the World on why they are who they are. But, if you explore the basic concept of choice, it seems to be the answer. Every life becomes an accumulation of choices made every second of every day … and the most powerful concept is how each and every one of us decides how to develop those choices. That is why I want to explore the concept of "choice … why it "haunted" me for years prior to picking up my pen to write down these thoughts. My guess is that this power within us is very telling of what the "right" choices are. Whether we listen, or not, is very telling about each and every one of us... a Universal concept, being the same for ALL of us …(except for those subjected to circumstances that most of us cannot even comprehend!).

One problem? Once we make a choice … there is no going back! Do you realize what an impact that has? And how many of us stop to realize the complete impact of that fact, once we have made a choice. Time does not erase itself … it only accumulates. So if we make a "wrong" choice, we cannot "undo" it, we can only make another choice to try to fix the first choice, (if we realize we made a wrong one). For an example, why would someone find themselves making the choice to marry over and over, thinking that "this" is the "right" one? My guess is that they did not realize the concept of choice. The power of choice is involved, whether the choice is right or wrong. If someone stopped to realize how much power is involved in choice, they would maybe stop making IRRATIONAL choices!

We can all "wish" things were different. The "power" is within us! My life has not always been the way I wanted it, and I could have made choices along the way that could have changed my entire life. With thyroid imbalance undiagnosed for years, then imbalance with other chemicals, because of the symptoms of the thyroid problem and not thinking normally because of it, over time, (for an example). Then add, the dynamic of a marriage. In every marriage, there is not one individual, but two people making choices, based on prior choices and experience … on a daily basis. If those choices do not blend, people "choose" to divorce. If this book could save even one marriage, and help each person understand the dynamic and power of choice, it would be a good thing, and I would be thankful that I kept pushing and pursuing to get this message to as many as will listen and learn and be receptive to the concept and power of choices and rational thinking!

To start at the beginning of my perception of "Choice". Most of us are born with a brain that works (and bless those otherwise). We start out, not realizing how the concept of choice works. It seems, though, that each of us develops the concept very early on … a child already has quite a definite idea of what they want from close to the beginning. As a parent, their responsibility by bringing this life onto this Earth, is to develop an understanding of the power of choice within that tiny being. Part of that "power" involves the difference between "right" and "wrong", and it is the responsibility of the "parent" to TEACH their children the difference between those two … "right" and "wrong". At an early age, to have those values instilled is the ultimate best. Anything less, results in the negative discourse in this World! A child who is taught those basics as a theme, with rational thinking, has a huge advantage.

What happens to a child, who has parents who do not realize, or care … about what they teach their child. What if they have no concept of the power of choice. They may be busy making the wrong choices, themselves, because maybe they were never taught. They may be injured, broken "children", having children themselves. How can a child realize their power of choice, if they are not taught by their parents, or their school, or their church, or their social worker?

Most people do not stop to realize such a basic concept. Therefore, most children are not taught the basic power within them!

It is a CHOICE to be a victim or a survivor, no matter what circumstances you were born into, (except those incomprehensible circumstances referred to earlier … which rational choice would eliminate). It is a choice to do something with your life … to search for your purpose, and find it. To take action, or not. To succeed, or fail. To push forward … or stay stuck in the past. Every second of every day, for each and every one of us, involves CHOICE.

This concept of choice is UNIVERSAL. If every person could realize the power of choice, and then live each and every second of their day searching for the "right" choice, this would be a different World. One problem, though, is that there are so many people who do not even know what a "right" choice is, let alone be able to live it. I would only get frustrated if I thought that I could "change the World", because that is not realistic. What I can do, though, is explore the concept with anyone who "chooses" to read this book.

To step back and think about it, it seems so easy. We can choose to feel happy or sad. Or glad or mad. So why do we choose to get upset with our husband or children, as an example? It could be …. I may have not eaten enough, often using coffee as my morning "meal"… not the best choice. Then projecting less than a desirable mood towards my family, not being the best choice that I could make. The possibilities of choices, on a daily basis, is so wide ranging. And can have such a huge impact on a family, over time, influencing the complexity of life.

garbage in ...
garbage out ....

examples of rationality
and irrationality

War is Irrational.

Rational would be each person focusing on their own thoughts, making them positive. Then focusing on family, and their special gifts to offer the World. Peace and Calm would follow.

Hate and Violence is disguised hurt and pain and sadness! Taking responsibility for our own happiness, severing our past, looking at our thoughts, and making them positive. Finding our Passion, then practice and study, then offer it to the World.

So much of each society, all over the World, is irrational. The Rich getting richer ...while people walk around homeless ... "Survival of the Fittest". For Centuries. The American public was certainly divided this past election ... on so many levels. Some of what happened was laughable, yet sad (that starving people have to watch the millions spent on the ads, for example...).

As we think more rationally, the results will follow. I studied "Rational Thinking" for two years .... and, have been practicing it, on a daily basis ... for more than twelve years now ... wow! It feels like my total approach to life is different, from what it was before. I intend to continue writing about this .... it can make a huge difference, as people learn more, and then teach their children, and others.

In confronting a thought .....then analyzing it to see "what" you are thinking?

*   Positive or Negative?

•   Constructive or Destructive?

•   Dealing with your Own Life?

       Or your Children …......

       Or, Someone's Business that is NOT Your's...

What Are You Thinking?

Is it.....

Rational or Irrational?

In the Present, Past, or Future?

Do YOU have Control over It?
Or, is It out of YOUR Control?

Does It Harm Another, in any way? Then, STOP!

How will YOU React...

What will the RESULT be?

This may seem complicated, at first ..... please, do not get overwhelmed! Realize that this is an overview of some of the thought processes, to detect rational or irrational thoughts and behavior, in your life. The lives of others, unless they are your children, parents or close friends, or a relative, needing you .... please REMEMBER ... "YOUR life is YOUR Business ...." If it is someone else's life .....it is NONE OF YOUR BUSINESS .... "start worrying about yourself."

"Keep it simple" ..."do not OVERTHINK!" It will become a natural way of "being", over time, creating new results with your new-found rational and positive thoughts, and therefore, your CHOICES will CHANGE! Concentrated effort, in the beginning, to establish positive patterns, for Yourself, will create automatic responses .... after practice and time ....

One step at a time ....One day at a time ....One rational thought at a time .... One rational choice at a time .... "equals" CHANGE IN THE WORLD!

LOVE ....

what a concept ....

rational thinking – the basics

Studying "Rational Thinking", for almost two years, was only the beginning for me. It is a way of stepping back, from your own thoughts, (as you are having them).....to think through whether your thought is rational, or not? This is an extremely important step involved, when realizing the power of each and every CHOICE. To think through whether or not your thought is rational, based on this knowledge... is your power... or not? Each person, without even realizing it, has thoughts, and therefore, "choices" to make, constantly. We each decide, moment by moment, what choices we make, and therefore, how our life will be.

I, personally, studied Rational Thinking, in a class setting, with an expert, for almost two years, and after that? I felt like a "baby" in a "new World". With the new concept of controlling my own thoughts, it took concentration, at first, to retrain my mind and SEVER MY PAST. No longer of use to me, except the knowledge that I gained from living the experiences, learning from them, and tucking away any loving, special memories. Most people though, including myself, have a tendency to carry their past along with them, like a ball and chain around their ankle. If you let go, and start new tomorrow, you will be amazed at the differences you will notice.

To understand what Rational Thinking actually is, it is best to use examples to show the difference. In class, we had a graph, similar to the illustration below, to help identify whether the thought is rational, as it is "examined".

Thought:

Emotion involved?
Past involved?
Irrational Thought Involved? Anger felt?
Any sadness?
Is my thought influenced?
What is a better Rational thought?
Does it make sense?
What is the action?
What are the consequences?

At first, it all seems like a complex process to dissect every thought. As the concept is learned and practiced, (practice is required to learn the concept), it becomes more and more natural. As you become more aware of your thoughts, then learn and practice the process, you will be amazed at how much power you actually have . . . the POWER is in your CHOICES.

examples of rational and irrational

thinking and behavior

**write what you know, about
your life ..... to be irrational ......**

**examples of
rational and
      irrational behavior**

**write what you know,
about your life ....
to be rational ....**

is your thinking ....

rational? ....

or

irrational? ....

harm to others ....

in any way ....

is a ....

W R O N G

choice ....

all of the negativity ....

can only change ....

one choice at a time ....

one person at a time ....

every time ....

I find myself ....

having a negative thought ....

generating negative results .....

I change it! ....

the promotion of rational thinking

After reading this book, and realizing your POWER involving rational thinking, it is my intention to do all I can to spread this new concept to all ends of the World! It is my theory that if all of humanity had a common "guide", with common knowledge involving rational thinking, it would help towards uniting our oneness. Aside from race or religion, any right you may have as a human being, in whatever element you find yourself in, this new Guide with its' knowledge and enlightenment, it has the potential to enhance your life!

It is an ongoing process. And once you have severed the complicated past, only keeping special memories and all of the lessons learned, it will become more clear of what your purpose is? If you still do not know, keep searching and experimenting until you discover what your true purpose is?

Then, moving forward, with a conscious decision to think rationally, each of us has a responsibility to humanity to be a decent human being ... we all bleed the same color!

don't throw stones . . .

if you ....

live in a glass house . . .

The chaos in our society can start healing, with new effort towards a common goal, and towards oneness as humanity. With the beginning of this, hopefully, we can see the need for education, starting at a very young age, continuing throughout life, from preschools to libraries, to parent meetings, to jails, and counseling offices, the White House, United Nations, and every nation in between. In churches, business boardrooms, scouts, boys and girls clubs ... every outlet possible that we can educate and practice rational thinking and incorporate in our everyday thinking.

The knowledge is power in a positive direction, once realizing such irrationality in so much we live with on a daily basis, as it is now. The discord, when analyzed, is reaching dangerous levels, without an intervention such as this Guide involving a "rational" approach to life.

Schools have a tendency of not wanting to teach what "should" be taught at home. Taking the critical levels of irrationality in this World, I suggest we adopt "new thinking" outlined in this book, to begin a shift in overall thinking in a more rational direction. Even though the results would not be immediate, at least a shift towards universal learning of rational thinking and the power of choice, it would begin to decrease all of the irrationality in this World, leaving a more peaceful and content feeling throughout the World.

Learn this, then pass it on, in more ways than one . . .

S T O P ! ! !

giving your power..........

A W A Y ....

to others ....

(and .... money, food, alcohol, drugs, shopping, gambling, etc) learn this . . . .

then,

pass it on . . . .

in more ways than one . . . . .

intuition . . .
(including that "inner voice" . . .)

Even though I have been working with these thoughts and this concept for over twenty years, and even though I practice rational thinking on an ongoing basis, it does not always feel like I have a way to totally control and continuously monitor my "intuition", or ("that voice inside of my head"!) I am convinced that an ongoing connection is a very important element to maintaining rational thinking, with positivity. For some reason, personally at least, my "voice" has a tendency to often drift in a negative direction . . . I will find myself thinking thoughts involving something in my past, possibly involving someone who hurt me . . . . dragging my emotion, one more time, through the muck and negativity of my past, for example. Why? I will mentally step back, think through what my thoughts are . . . sometimes getting so irritated with myself for wasting that moment with such a wasteful thought that accomplishes nothing for myself! Do you know the feeling?

I am convinced that for myself, personally, it is important for me to keep my thought processes as positive as possible. It is a topic that is extremely important to me, yet I must be in such a minority on the subject. With what has evolved to being on television on a daily basis ... the movies released with violence, and all of the other negative qualities . . . with my theory of "garbage in, garbage out", relating to influence that I allow into my brain, I am definitely in the minority. As our society becomes more and more absorbed with negativity . . . . if my concern is valid, and if it is true that energy has influence, whether positive or negative, it is a huge concern with all of the negativity in this World.

With a new President, in the United States, it is symbolic of how we make choices, often without even realizing how we decide what that choice will be, along with the results... the benefits and/or consequences. There was so much negativity in the election, yet we are forced to accept the outcome. Intuition, that inner voice, told many people prior to the election that the results would be different. It shows that even though the intuitions of many said that the irrational and negative talk during the campaign would lose and a more mature, rational approach would win, it did not end up being the case. Why?

When I look at the concept of "intuition", it makes me wonder if I am correct with the belief that "positive in, positive out", "negative in, negative out"? To explain myself further, it is my belief that the constant exposure to the content of many television shows and video games is contributing to the delinquency of our society, at least in the United States. Maybe you would say that I choose to live in a "self induced bubble" ... as much as possible. And even attempting to filter myself and only allow positive into my life, I still struggle with "positive intuition". It is an ongoing monitoring process to keep myself "on the right track", and it is not just an automatic reaction for my intuition. Why?

No matter how much effort it is to keep myself "positive", with my intuition on a constant flow of positive input, it takes the desire to make that choice, in the first place. Then, whenever I realize that my "inner voice" and/or intuition is not in a positive place, I stop myself ... center my mind ... remind myself of my desire to be positive, no matter what the circumstances, and then I redirect my thoughts onto a more desirable direction, such as an overview of my goals and dreams.

I believe that my intuition/inner voice plays a large contributing part in me accomplishing my dreams. If I am spending my moments thinking negatively about someone and/or something, with judgment or mismanaged thoughts, it does not help my forward motion, because it usually involves my past, with its' many mistakes. Then, the same amount of time that I could have spent counseling myself concerning my forward motion, I have wasted the same moment!

common sense

What a concept? If "common sense" was a concept that was taught to young children, from a very early age, and if it was a "common theme" in all societies around the World, slowly the overall desire of ALL would become the better GOOD of each and every person on this planet. Why we think that destruction, war, oppression, poverty, etc., is the way of life, is misguided and misinformed. It is reality that entire societies only know these negative elements that exist, so the negative teaches negative and so on it goes. My desire, with this book, is to begin to share a glimmer of hope for people who have not had hope in the past. Tomorrow can be a new day, for ALL of us, as we share together in pushing forward to use Common Sense, for the better good of ALL.

Common Sense is the realization that we are all in this together. "Common" means the loss of the need to only be individual, and the desire to put energy and effort towards the good of ALL. If each of us took care of ourselves, and were taught how to do that, it would also be a good direction to teach the importance of caring for others. For one thing, when you care for another, the feeling it brings is a charge of positive energy to boost you. Done over and over, it builds upon itself ... proving to be a good influence for anyone involved. When positive energy is directed towards others, ALL benefit.

I urge anyone reading this, and then those sharing with others, to include Common Sense as one of the topics discussed. Illustrations of common sense did not always shine in the past, to say the least. Moving forward, with a universal concept of positivity . . . common sense and level thinking towards what is rational should be an ongoing question for all on an ongoing basis.

success

Success is universal … with many different definitions. It is almost always used to define monetary value. We say, "if someone is rich, they are "successful". Many times, though, money has nothing to do with success! If that rich person is happily married, spends quality time with their children, and has peace of mind, for example, if they are happy … THEN, in my opinion, that would be my definition of "success"… not ONLY because of his monetary value. That is not often the case, though. Often, a person who is driven to become "rich", (financially), spends most of their time, energy and passion on that drive. I would not necessarily say that is success. A poor person (financially) can be "successful", if that is their choice, and they align themselves with positive thoughts and ways to interact with life. Although a "poor" person is usually so busy dealing with the elements of survival, they can make a decision to live a "rich" life, realizing that money is not the only thing that makes a person happy and "successful".

Taking the concept of "choices" into consideration, success is a measure of the accumulation of positive choices with positive results. It includes the right mindset, knowledge and desire … then one choice at a time. Over a period of time . . . building upon itself, until the results show positive results, an individual makes thousands of choices every day, and knowing that those choices, altogether, determine success or failure in your life. Knowing this, and realizing the power of this realization, will hopefully shift your thinking towards positive choices moving forward. This, if nothing else, can make a huge impact in your life and the way you spend your time.

Possibly, just realizing the power you have within you, and your power of choice, will cause you to want to analyze where you are at in your life. Where you have been because of the choices you have made in your past ... then, severing the negativity and developing the desire to only involve positivity moving forward in the overall ongoing "theme" of your life. If each person concentrated in putting goodness into the World, over time, it would become a more peaceful place to live ... in your own community ... to the overall theme of each and every person ...

Money is only one aspect, there are many aspects of "success" that cannot be measured. If we would start accumulating our successes in everything we do, rather than having "success" only being related to money, and an ultimate goal, rather than realizing the important process, we would not feel like such "failures" if we do not have a lot of money. For some reason, over time, especially the American culture, that people with money "have it", and people without don't, the judgment would begin to lessen, as it should. Although negativity often accompanies the lack of money, it does not mean that all people who do not have money are not successful. Life circumstances can be harsh, and more empathy and less judgment from those who do have money would be a desirable direction for all of us. No matter what, there will always be those that have more, and those who have less. If we could only move in the direction of thinking about helping others more, and wanting less ourselves along with dishing out less judgment, our World would be a better place for all.

People who do not have money have a tendency to feel like such failures. Life is not an automatic birth right of "having" . . . those born without have extremely difficult adversity to overcome. If our directions become themed with helping each other, and helping lessen the gap between haves and have not's, we will ALL become better because of it.

successful

An example of how I feel "successful" in my life, without having a lot of money, the way my children have evolved is extraordinary ! Yes, they have made "right" choices along the way . . . my son's "choice" of a wife, for example, is perfect for all of us . . . what more could a mother ask for. Not to say that I have had my times along the way, that I have not been the "perfect mother", and sometimes my children were taking care of me. But overall, and the times that neither of them remember, are the thousands of hours of patience, love, teaching, time and effort determined to bring the two responsibilities called children, that I brought into this World ... successful children do not "just happen". They are my "walking rewards" for the time in my life, from the moment they were born until now ...a sense of pride that only a mother knows.

My children were my "career", for a long time, and having them be successful and happy ... that is MY success! (Although I am judged as "nothing", because I barely make money, now, being totally behind with technology, and having to begin again). If I cared about that "judgment", which I used to, it would totally affect my self-esteem . . . my husband and family being my worst critics. Luckily, I have no regrets ... I would do it exactly the same if I were to do it again, which is a very good feeling. There is nothing like a successful child, watching them maneuver this World with a command that I could not even imagine. Without the base that they received as children, I am convinced that a child has a much less chance at having such inner strength, without that inner base of love from within. Their success is my success.

A mother, who has a great career, who is earning a wonderful salary, but who has children who do not function well in society? All of the money in the world cannot bring back the time a child needs to learn from a mother, (or important, loving care provider... not just another child in a class of many). A child is a child, they grow up so fast, and it can make such a difference in their lives, whether a child is a "success" or a "problem child"? A career, for a mother, can be extremely rewarding, and may fulfill them as a person. Also, some caregivers, in the right circumstances can be as good or better as the involvement with a mother. So my words involve some or many, not all. A mother, especially a single mother, who is forced to work, just to survive for her and her child/children ... of course my words are not directed at them. Some circumstances involve extremely difficult adversity. If real quality time is spent with your child, in one way or another, the teaching and love is the most important, and no judgment is intended or implied ... what worked for me may not be an option for some. For the mother who chooses to bring a child into the world, and then chooses to go back to their career after six weeks, to continue their own career, giving up all of those special moments with their child ... each mother, (or significant care provider), has so many choices involved in raising a child. To begin with, for the mother, creating that child in the first place. Once conceived, that responsibility is not an option . . . it happens one way or another, then there is another person living on this planet. Their thoughts and beliefs have a huge amount to do with how they interacted with their mothers, (or significant care provider), from the very beginning.

The same is true about fathers. For the father, who can balance a career and still spend quality time with their child/children, they have the opportunity for two successes in their lives. For the father who is "so busy" achieving that they do not have the time or desire to spend quality time with their child, they do not realize the "true meaning" of fatherhood.

Marriages are either "successful" ... or not. In every situation, there is not one opinion, there are two opinions, from two different backgrounds, attempting to move their combined ways through every detail of life, and I applaud anyone who can accomplish that in a "successful" way.

Some marriages are "successful" because, as a unit of one, they make a conscious decision to be that way. Then they figure out ways to work upon the strengths of each, and compensate each other for the differences. Some know that no matter what, they will always be married, loving each other with this approach and sureness, working through their differences and learning how to create an environment good for themselves and each other. If they are committed to making positive choices in their lives, separately and together, it has a lot to do with the results they receive. With a delicate balance, "success" is a concept measured every single day.

Success comes from within. Peace comes from within. Love comes from within. It is that "pat on the back", when we do something well that helps ... that "inner voice" saying, "good job, you did it!" And, just because I am not a success, monetarily ... (yet), or had some "failures", or maybe not the life that others in my life had in mind for me, it is an inner measure in myself that matters ... nothing else. Just because I am not a "success" in my life, financially, does not make me a failure.

I have finally given myself permission, and the freedom, of not having to be "perfect". And, I started thinking of myself as a "success"! I have categorized my own life into every aspect that is important to ME. I keep an ongoing evaluation of my "success rate", and I do not "beat myself up" if I am not succeeding in an area ... I just concentrate on what I have to do, and the actions I need to take, to accomplish what I want to. I concentrate on what I HAVE accomplished, and in a very positive way, attempt to strive to achieve my goals.

My goals and aspects of my life that are important to me, may be completely different from your choices. No one can tell you what "should" be important to you, that is your choice, depending on your circumstances, beliefs and values. Your success rate is your own, and no one can tell you that you are a failure, especially society (or your family). The main thing is that "success breeds success ... failure and that attitude brings more failure". If you are constantly being told that you are a failure, and you are constantly feeling like a failure, it will affect your self-esteem and eat away at your inner- strength and positive attitude.

If you can break down your life, mentally, into many small pieces, and concentrate on being successful ... one piece at a time, you will begin to see that you are a success in many ways. Stop striving for perfection and be thankful for the many ways that you are a success. Especially, stop only relating your success rate by looking at your bank account. Yes, it is a measure. Yes, money is a very important element in your quality of life, in many ways. When you start looking at yourself in a more positive way, it will increase your inner strength, and give you the "power" of CHOICE, to be the "success" that you want to be, one step at a time, in so many ways.

Just have a dream, (or several), keep moving forward ... SEVER the past, and "just do it" ...

read this book ....

then,

pass it on .....

in more ways .....

than one ....

growing up

In my life, I was so fortunate to have two parents, who loved me, and loved each other for more than fifty years. I was a huge part of my family and made to feel very special and important. I know my parents well, and although my father has passed on, my mother and I share a closeness difficult to compare. One of my sisters, on the other hand, to hear her tell of her childhood, it would seem that she had two completely different parents, and a completely different experience in our family. She was the oldest, I was the youngest. I was able to learn from her mistakes, (that she does not remember), that completely impacted our family for a very long time. Luckily, from the depths of some very dark places, each of us has evolved in our own, separate ways. Amazing, though, that perception of reality is one of the most important elements in shaping which choices we make in life. And often, the choices and results, starting at exactly the same place, can be completely opposite, depending on who you are and what your perception is....which is based on an accumulation of prior choices, education, experience, and your exclusive uniqueness.

One thing I would like to explore, is "why" we make the choices we do. How did it happen that my sister perceive her life in our family, with the same parents, in such an opposite way from how my other sister and I did. Along the way, I was always taught to listen to my inner voice and that intuition inside myself, whispering in my ear. Diversity comes because every person on this Earth has a different "voice".

A question that I have had for a very long time, is, "why are the voices so different, and often so negative?" And one theory that I have, is that it makes a huge amount of difference how a child is interacted with, from the very beginning. Those bonds and connections, in my opinion, have an impact in the ongoing choices people make, even as children, and throughout their lives. Being taught right from wrong, positive and negative, and some insight into consequences, from the very beginning ... makes a big difference, in my opinion. Also, food allergies, chemical imbalance, and many other factors, of all kinds, can also change behavior.

If we could embrace a new and different approach of incorporating rational thinking and the knowledge of the power of choice into our teaching, in all ways, at all levels. As time goes on, I plan to keep learning as much as I possibly can relating to those new concepts. There have been such important influences, along the way ... classes and counselors that have taught me so much. For those children, though, born into less than a loving, two parent, middle class, American family ... never being taught? No matter what background, with the basic elements contained in this book, each and every person can have an opportunity to accept, then change who they are and how they are. That is a powerful concept ... that with a widespread, consistent, common knowledge involving choice and rational thinking, the World can be a different place to live ... eventually ... with evolved thinking.

If we slowly introduce this Guide to the different sources for people in the World, in schools, churches, jails, etc., as people introduce themselves to the entire concept that I am discussing . . . the life changing process that I went through ... it has taken years, for myself, to feel a comfort zone with the power within me, and how to best use it to my advantage. Sometimes, we become our own worst enemy ....having the best intentions, and yet sabotaging ourselves with procrastination, or gossip, or other negativity ... learning that positivity makes such a huge difference in our choices is a key element in promoting our desire to change.

It seems like we are all so busy trying to get through the day, that we do not stop long enough to consider "how" we are living? We grow up a little more, each day, but what does that mean?

We may "grow older", but do we "grow wiser"? Or are we just so busy doing our best to "function", that we do not realize our individual choices, and the thought processes behind the "why". For every choice, there is a "why", never even realized, for most of us, for most of our lives … unless we come along someone, like I did, that introduced me to the concept of rational thinking. It is one reason why I want to share this message with as many people as possible, since it changed my life so completely.

We all have a tendency to rush off to work, possibly late, stuck in traffic, irritable … to begin our day, possibly without eating … a cup or three of coffee … sound familiar? Do we ever stop to think of the power we have of our thoughts, as we function throughout our day? We DO have the power of choice, including our thought processes, our traveling routes we take, and how much time we give ourselves to get where we need to work. Planning, and realizing that taking back a lot of our power, can make a difference in our stress levels, and therefore, our health. Frustration and anger, compared to peace of mind … over time, remember? Negative equals negative, and positive promotes positive. So how can someone expect to be happy and good if they are having road rage on the way to work, for example? Listening to peaceful music while planning out the day … productive. Screaming at drivers in front of you and getting frustrated because you are late … promoting negativity, without even realizing.

We have the choice, for example, whether we comfort and teach our children, or walk in yelling at them. Hopefully, you are getting a glimpse of what I am saying … a person who had a difficult day, who experienced frustration and road rage, it would be very difficult to turn that emotion off while walking in the door, to greet your children with, "how was your day"? "Go play", and how are they to feel that connection and love, with a parent who is acting angry and negative … who may ease their pain with alcohol or drugs, for example. Like a snowball, positive or negative, what is YOUR choice? Do you stop to think about your reaction with your children, and the impact that your words and actions, (or lack of), may have?

With the constant interaction with technology that parents seem to need recently, it is not even known, yet, what impact that will have on society over a period of time. Children need to be talked to, and interacted with, to develop their thought process necessary to make powerful choices moving forward. If parents continue to pay more attention to their technology rather than their children, we will eventually end up with a society that just does not know differently, because they were never taught. This book is an attempt to counteract that downward spiral.

This book is an attempt to get people to wake up, just a bit. It feels like there has already been a revolution happening, and yet it seemed to have such a negative twist. Now, we have a new leader in the Western World . . . Donald Trump, President of the United States, there is a new energy developing and only the future. Each of us has a powerful new beginning, if we approach this Democratic process with an open mind and realize that our choices can keep a large majority of the American public stuck in such a negative state. Or, along with the Trump supporters, we can embrace the system and the country we live in. Beyond that, the power of the people has spoken. Time will tell, whether this book, and it's concept, can make a difference in this confusion we find ourselves in? I certainly hope so.

A glimpse into a future book I will be writing … "if I only had known, I would have made different choices, and my life would have been different …" … the book's name:

("Choices …. evolved …")

"If I only knew then, what I know now …"

I had to be "taught", after becoming an adult ….

RATIONAL THINKING

+ INTUITION

*and teaching our inner voice to be Positive ...

+

LOVE

=

A CHANGED WORLD

marriage

Marriage is such an accepted part of life. And when you look at the entire concept of marriage, in a rational way, such a unique choice to make. It usually starts with friendship, compassion, respect, and all of the elements that most people want from life and a partner. So why do so many marriages evolve into hate, disrespect, disagreement, and often end in divorce? How can two people start out in such a positive way and allow themselves to change their feelings, over time?

Moving forward, if marriage could include more "rational thinking", and eliminate a lot of the selfish negativity, a marriage would possibly have a chance. Walking into a marriage, like I did … to a First Sergeant in the United States Army …absolutely NO possibility that there could possibly be anything he could be responsible for destroying, (like my self-esteem). I had no concept of my own power, and he was driven to dominate my already fragile ego. Without learning about rational thinking, we would have had no possibility of success with our marriage. Luckily, I was willing to be counseled by a brilliant counselor who taught me about myself and my marriage and ways to turn obstacles into ways to interact in special ways. I would highly recommend as many ways of learning about yourself and your partner, especially in a marriage situation, to move forward on "the same page".

In many circumstances, positive turns into negative, then keeps evolving in a negative direction, once it starts in that direction. Without realizing what is happening, often, each partner adopts a theory of what is wrong with the OTHER person, taking no responsibility for what is happening. Without guidance, knowledge and insight into what is happening, it is often to repair the destruction, once it starts. The main thing to offer with this new knowledge, that there is always more than one choice.

Marriage needs to be a combination and a blend of choices. If there is a decision to be made, it should be a combination of both points of view, that result in the decision on behalf of the marriage. If, over time, one or the other partner starts making decisions without consulting the other partner, and if the other partner does not agree with the decisions being made, it can become the beginning of resentment and misunderstanding. Communication makes a huge difference in a marriage, and a willingness to bend and flow with your partner through a world of compromise. I am convinced that rational thinking would also enhance any marriage, no matter how happy you are. The knowledge and ability to analyze and comprehend rational thinking is just an additional way to keep growing as an individual, growing as a person, and as part of a marriage.

With a common and conscious effort, by both parties of a marriage, the potential is incredible. One way to comprehend some of the complexity involved is to understand it. To realize and comprehend and have the knowledge of the elements of rational thinking gives the partners a simple and common way to relate to each other in an effective way. When you consider how many decisions are involved in a marriage, with two different opinions affecting each decision, no wonder there is a lot of conflict and confusion within marriage, leading to misunderstanding, resentment, and ultimately divorce. Possibly with new knowledge involving rational thinking and choices, the rate of divorce may start reversing and allow partners to develop ongoing ways to relate to each other.

Hopefully, you can see the complexity involved with one persons' choices. And marriage involves two, plus any children born into the marriage. Then, the dynamic among each other and the interaction with the children, no wonder there are complications, at times.

Can you see the power of the choices each person, in a marriage, makes as an ongoing "process" necessary for an ongoing success in a marriage. One small choice leads to another, and another, and another. Hopefully, over time . . . especially in a marriage, both partners will flow with the choices made, and not feel resentful. If anyone reading this can relate to "marriage", if they can relate to how many choices are involved from day to day for a marriage, maybe you can relate that there is no "right" choice to any situation, unless it is "right" for both of you!

It is easy for family and friends to all develop an "opinion" as to "what is best", or so they say. They can voice their reactions and what they would do . . . tell you what you should do. Always remember, though, no matter who is telling you what … "if they are not walking in your shoes, they have no idea, and it is none of their business". It is easy to sway back and forth, depending on who you are talking to and/or listening to. Hopefully, the parties will remember, though, that they are married to each other, and not all of the external "noise". At the end of the day, only the ones involved in the marriage, from their own individual perspectives, can relate to the ongoing progress of the marriage.

No one can predict the future. Every marriage has different circumstances, and involve two individuals who had their own set of circumstances before coming to the marriage. At least by being exposed to the concept of rational thinking, and realizing the potential in a marriage, it is exciting to share the exciting direction for the future. To recognize that neither party has a majority, all choices are negotiable, and each person deserves to be heard, and deserves comfort within the marriage. If that is not the case, you at least have the responsibility, to the other person, to be honest. It is an unspoken "rule" in marriage to do whatever it takes to "make it work". For some marriages, partners are able to adapt and compromise to suit each other and themselves. In other marriages, the differences become too great, and over time, the connection breaks down, resulting in the large divorce rate. If attention was paid to the individual choices made, to begin with, and a plan and program was developed for the marriage, (from the very beginning is the best), and it could possibly make a difference. Then, if developed by both people, there will be equal pride in the forward progress of the marriage, and each can compromise and adjust as needed. With individual opinions working WITH each other to "make it work", it ends up developing a "life of it's own".

Most people do not fall in love and decide to marry, with all of the details on their minds. And, maybe they should consider the complexity from the beginning. As time goes on, and as choices are made, both individually and together as the marriage, sometimes the people involved become closer and more in love. Others, though, start wondering who they really are ... and who did they marry? I highly recommend a common code of honesty within marriage. Bringing your authentic self from the very beginning is so important, not only for yourself, but for the other person. It is not right to marry one person, having them change their overall character once you say, "I do". If you go into marriage with an open mind, and the desire to change along with your partner, rather than fighting the union and striving for independence within the marriage. The dynamic is complex to begin with, and being informed and knowledgeable about rational thinking and the power of choice can certainly enhance the day to day, moment by moment dealings within a marriage.

"will it enhance my life? . . .

family

We do not have a choice when it refers to "Family". We do not have a choice of who our Mother and Father will be. I was fortunate enough to be born into the most loving, secure, wonderful family. Some people are born into the opposite circumstances, or anything in between. We may not have a choice of who our parents are, or the circumstances we are born into. We do, though, have a choice of who we become . . . recognizing that the path each person takes is certainly not the same.

A person born into an extremely wealthy family, for example, may have a fast forward track to college or many of the "perks" of having money. They also "inherit", though, for example … the personality and character of that family. We all know of situations in wealthy circumstances, (or at least seen in movies), where children are raised by nannies and sent away to boarding schools … barely actually knowing their parents, who are too busy for their children.

For another example, we have also seen circumstances where children come from the depths of poverty, the father barely recognizes his child, struggle is a normal way of life. Yet, for the example, the mother is the most loving example of a person for her child, she works to feed them, then shares her time reading and loving and teaching. Although poor, the child grows up feeling loved and pushes for scholarships and succeeds in college and life. The rich child, to continue this example, off at boarding school, stays in trouble most of the time. They get involved with smoking and drinking alcohol, because they have not been taught differently, and they waste their education away, not paying attention because they have no respect for the privilege, never having to struggle for anything. They end up with no social class and after burning bridges with their family, they end up on the street.

Of course, these are extreme examples of opposite situations that start with the birth of an innocent child. Every child starts this life needing help, with hopefully at least one adult who cares about not only their day to day functioning, but also, hopefully they have some loving, caring people around them who teach them right from wrong, good from bad, love from hate, etc. The basics of life are so extremely important to a child, from the very beginning. It is amazing how fast a child develops their basic belief system, and input from their closest adults is essential to establishing the foundation that child will need in life.

Then, depending on the circumstances of a child, they will go to school. What setting that is, when they start, and who their teachers will be? After being exposed to the knowledge in this book, I hope you are starting to realize how many variables go into each and every life on this Earth . . . and how choices, chosen for you in the beginning and then up to each person, every moment of every day … does anyone stop to realize how these choices end up formulating who each child becomes. Some people may ponder the overall theme of having conscious thought. Few, I am sure, stop often to realize how their thoughts and beliefs and choices, accumulated, end up formulating who they become.

Each person born has a clean state of mind, to begin with. And the accumulation of choices begins immediately, even though they are made by other people at the start. Very early on, a child decides some of what they want for their choices … and become more complex and sure as time goes on. What we learn as children, good and bad, carries with us throughout our adult lives. Unfortunately, some people do not always experience the best of circumstances, and that also carries with them. With the knowledge of "rational thinking", and the "power of choices", and knowing that choice can be changed at any time, maybe not easily, but it can be done.

Knowing that rational thinking can renew our thoughts and free us of any burdens, due to any negativity in the past. When we move through life with rational thought, it reminds us that we have the power of our choice, no one else … not family, not friends, not our co-workers … influence makes a difference in our analysis of our thoughts and choices, but we have the ultimate power to decide and make choice. If we come from a loving family environment, you would think that you would have an advantage. Not necessarily. As in my case, I was so loved and protected and innocent, that when I started interacting with "life", it took some disappointment and "tough knocks", many times, because life is not always as loving as my mother and father were/are. I had to learn to "protect" myself from much of the overwhelming, unfair situations I would find myself in. It took classes, reading, and soul searching … I had some extremely brilliant counselors that changed my life. Each of us make our own way, and make our own choices as we go. What I had to learn, as I went along, is that the power of choice is not always as clear, as it seems.

Whether you are out in life, or in the comfort of your special environment, choices are always involved. Family, with their beliefs and traditions, for the base where we come from. Then, as we grow up, and learn to make our own choices … our life becomes more of our own. Unfortunately, though, as we move into making more and more of our own choices, without knowing our own power, many times we let others make choices for us. Take the example of college students drinking alcohol. Look at the "choice" facing so many young adults … do what friends do? Did your parents teach you anything about alcohol? Does alcoholism, the disease, run in your family? Do you know that one night of drinking can change your life, as you know it? So many factors go into each choice, and at times, as in this example, many teens and young college students let others make choices for them! At the least, if we started teaching children the power of choice at very young ages, from different sources rather than relying learning about choice only from family, at least that teen would know of rational thinking prior to following someone into a wrong choice!

That is only one example. And, I am hoping that you are starting to see that choice is involved so much in our lives. Hopefully, also, you are realizing that you can create a "clean slate", at any time. To "sever the past", it gives the freedom from past experience that has a negative impact on you. And, it allows you to begin new ways, if you are not pleased with the direction your choices are taking you. Sometimes, we get stuck in a direction, based on choices that our family or friends have chosen for us. Or, we get stuck in a rut, making choices based on chemical addiction, and the "roller coaster" that creates in your personality. So many variables on such an ongoing basis, end up formulating who we are and how we are, and therefore, how people interact with us. My hope is that by opening your mind to this new and unique concept, that you have the option to think rationally, and make conscientious choices … as we move through time, called life.

It seems like, so often, we carry around the "extra baggage", accumulating our choices, right and especially "wrong" ones, feeling worse and worse, reacting more and more negatively, and we may not even realize why. Do you realize the POWER you have, to make the decision to start over? You can DECIDE to be different, then, your actions and reactions can be whatever you want them to be. Most of us move through life not realizing this concept. We "just go along", first with our family … then with our college friends … then with our co-workers and our spouses' friends. Does this sound familiar? Do you ever stop to realize "why" you "function" the way you do? Does it occur to you that each and every moment involves CHOICE?

If we can start beginning to educate our children, at an earlier age, that they need to start becoming aware of their "options" of choice, and make as many moments, as possible, to become "teaching moments". If we start integrating these concepts of rational thinking and the power of choice into our schools, introducing the elements of pause to think before acting … as children would grow and develop their own lives, they would realize that slowly people would change. They would start being more aware of how their choices affect others. And, they would be working on themselves and their own circle of family and friends, rather than worrying so much about what is wrong with others.

My hope, is that families would become more and more the nurturing and teaching nucleus that children truly need, not just, "go out and play", but realizing that if we teach our children, we change the World! There is such a difference between "teaching" our children, and "just letting kids be kids". An example that I have of that … one child that was "taught" ended up being in Special Forces in the United States of America. The child that was told to just go be a kid and play, with not a lot of respect for the intelligence a child has at such an early age, ended up in jail. Not to say that all examples will end this way, far from it … brilliant people have come from extremely adverse conditions and childhoods. I am just hoping to bring awareness to each person who may read this book … and hopefully the message will spread to the point of making a difference in this World.

Many times, people will allow their past to define them. And their family members become their "judge and jury". What gives family members "permission" to gossip, decide, and come to a final judgment about another family member? Done in the name of love? Sometimes, their thoughts and feelings can totally paralyze a person, without them even realizing. Many times, a person will actually care about what people think about them, right? Especially your Mother or Father? What happens to your self-esteem if you listen to that judgment? Well, along with everything else … no matter what, it is YOUR choice if you ALLOW their thoughts or feelings, right and/or wrong, to affect YOU! Do you see? Yes … it matters when you are younger, growing up. But, from the time you become an adult, you have the power to "let it go". You no longer HAVE to listen to your parents' opinion or judgment. You can live your life, filtering your own positive thoughts, not allowing any negativity to affect any choice that you make. Easy to say, difficult to do? Yes, especially if you love your parents and their opinion goes straight to your soul.

Adversity, no matter how it comes to us, builds strength and character, and defines what really matters to us. If we allow outside influences to dictate what our choices will be, over time, it will gnaw at us like a cancer. We are our own best barometer of what is best for ourselves. And often what happens, especially with a soft spirited person … allowing others to live YOUR life, it will become "telling", in one way or another. In a marriage, if your spouse makes choices for you, against your grain. In families, if a father or mother starts making decisions for the family that irritate their partner … so many variables, they all result in choices … good or bad … right or wrong … what might be right for one, may be wrong for the other. If we can only become more aware of our own choices, then, maybe a little more aware of how we affect others, and how others affect us … we can move in a forward direction. This common knowledge can make a big difference in the overall dynamics of families … rational thinking makes a HUGE difference in everything, especially choices.

One huge challenge we face, now, is the overwhelming amount of technology available to all of us, on an ongoing basis. When I was raised, we were a lucky one to have a black and white television. Then, one day, COLOR came to our living room, and we were changed. The television shows became more and more developed, I would sneak out to watch "Wagon Train" with my Dad. Today, with computers, video games, violence, magic, etc, etc, our children have exposure to so much negative in life without us even realizing. Even with parents that do their best to filter the information, then there is the risk that their children will search and "learn" the wrong things from the wrong people. Such an ongoing element to manage, and figure out a balance to give your children age appropriate choices, without having them exposed to the negative, not meant for childrens' eyes and minds.

As we learn more about the power of choice, and the concept of rational thinking to make those choices, we will hopefully evolve into a more thoughtful society with some more depth. Children having children has been a problem, but as we learn from a very early age, our power to make the choice to say, "no", or that we have the power to choose who we spend time with, or that just because we were born into a circumstance with parents who made wrong choices, does not mean that we need to continue those patterns. Severing a negative past, or savoring a positive one … each person has the option of deciding "what" about them are the elements that define them. When I realized this, and the fact that I could pick and choose what memories I keep, which memories I eliminate because they are toxic to me … it frees up my mind to give me the most potential of being a positive person.

It seems so simple, sitting here writing with the knowledge, years of practice and hindsight. Believe me, from the point that I was introduced to these concepts of rational thinking and the power of choice, until now? Years and years of practice, on a daily basis …. not a difficult thing, just a decision to take control of my ongoing choices, with positive input and rational thinking weaved throughout, and I am like a different person. Why did I not learn this sooner, my life would have been different! It was never taught to me, either by my parents, or my school. I lived through life trying to please everyone, and never felt like I did. My self-esteem suffered because I made choices to boost other people, which continued to happen, which was fine. But what about me? It was not my parent's fault, they had no idea. They lived their lives, to the best of their ability, and bless them for the love and kindness they always have shown to me. Evolving in life, though, I stumbled upon some concepts that changed my life forever. That is what I attempt to share with you, and urge these concepts to become forefront on a Universal level . . . rational thinking would change everything, and is not especially common, as things are now.

We begin our lives with a clean slate. And the complexity of life changes who we are from a very early age. If we were all exposed to rational thinking, from a very early age, it would make a difference for everyone, moving forward. To recognize that something needs to change … the violence and discourse in this World is frightening. Stopping to realize what we are doing, and asking "why"? Then, if each of us could take responsibility for ourselves, and stop thinking so much about others … there is no way to have every answer to all of what is happening. Just thinking about what we think and why, though, and the influences we allow into our lives … positive will always overcome negative … that would be one belief that could start making changes, with action.

do I like who I am .....

do I want to be my "lazy self" …

do I want to accomplish my purpose …

family

Marriages become broken, at times, so what happens to their children? No wonder there is so much chaos in this World. Hearts get broken, families become broken, and then we expect our children to turn out "normal". What is "normal". There are so many different combinations when defining "family", so at this point, anywhere in the World ... any way you consider family, is family. Some adults, though, are broken from their own childhoods, then have children, expecting "normal". If we can gain new understanding, like I did along the way, that we each have a responsibility to ourselves, to make sure that we realize our own power, with our choices. If we practice rational thinking to evolve into the person we were meant to be, accomplishing our passion to contribute at an ultimate capacity to offer this World our unique gifts. The diversity is what makes it all work. And, remembering the power within us, makes it that much better!

It begins with the knowledge of the "power" of choice. It begins with us learning and believing that there is more than one alternative or option, in almost every circumstance. Believing that you call upon your background, and use it in a way that will be positive. If you had a difficult beginning ... rather than being paralyzed by it as you grow up, you have the choice to sever it, and learn from it, and move on. If we had a wonderful beginning, we can utilize our background, if you want, to influence and mentor others that were not so fortunate, if you choose to, as an example. Or you can choose to bully those less fortunate . . . positive to negative, and many choices inbetween. Do you begin to see how the concept of choice, rational thinking by realizing your initial reaction to a situation, then pausing ... stepping away to pause and think through your interaction to that thought … it may seem too involved? Over time, it becomes so natural that you do not even realize the process you are going through, and yet, you put together a string of positive, good choices that you have chosen, rather than impulse reactions that you do not like for yourself.

Knowing that you call upon your past is good to know. How you move forward in your life, with or without your "blood relatives", realizing that sometimes friends are more loving towards you. Some family, just like marriages, figure out ways to support rather than judge, and to live their own lives rather than thinking that they know what is better for you, more than you do … then gossiping about it, and deciding what is right or wrong for YOU. You can move forward, regardless of their opinions, you can still love them, love yourself, love who you are and how you are. The more you learn how to make these choices, rather than surrendering to their opinion, the better you will feel. You have the right, that you earned by birth right, to have the ultimate opinion of what you do, how you feel, and how you act in life. The opinion of others is just that, their opinion. One key to moving forward is not only to "sever the past". But to forgive and accept what happened, as you leave behind any negativity that was part of it, and find a special place in your heart for all of the positive, cherished memories.

Before moving on, I want to utilize an example of a "typical" family situation . . . two working parents, two children in elementary school, after school care, sports, Church, and then expect to manage a "relationship". The parents are stressed because of their work, and they do not make enough to cover all of the bills, then sports needs uniforms, cupcakes on Saturday, the Church has a potluck on Sunday and the father has deadlines on Friday, that take ALL of his attention. The mother starts resenting having to work, plus parent, plus carpool, plus laundry and housework, while the husband thinks that doing his work is the only important thing for the family, which it is so that he does not lose his job. They take turns picking the kids up from daycare, with too much traffic going home.

In this example, I hope that it seems so ridiculous that you just laugh. The problem is that it may be true for you? Or a similar situation … you may not even be able to find a job. Then, you have children who constantly need attention, whether you have patience or not. They have no idea that you have bills to pay, with no money. They have no idea that you cannot stand your partner, at the moment, because of building stress without resolving issues along the way. So you are about ready to explode, and your child is saying, "Mommy, do you want to play or read me a book?"   What do you think your initial reaction will be? "NO...." right? If you could only step back and realize that children are so vulnerable and much of what they absorb is channeled through how you react to them. They have no idea what you are going through, and they do not realize that the pressure of the world is on your shoulders. They only see your reaction, and if you can step back and think rationally … over a period of time, you will see a difference … as you become aware of rational thinking and the power of choice, and as your choices involve interaction with your child, you will start feeling better. Not overnight, possibly, but a shift in the theme of negativity, can have a huge impact on a child. And, you have the power of change, anytime you make the decision, or choice, to do so.

People end up in the most complex, unusual, uncomfortable circumstances, at times. Then, their children automatically become involved, being an extension of their parents. If the adults in the family do not realize the impact of their actions have on children, they act and react, watching violence in front of their children, for example, and wonder why their children become negative and violent. The more aware of what a child is exposed to, from an early age, makes a difference in who they become.

It is my hope, that the more aware people become at the impact of their actions, and how it affects their children, that they will have more desire to interact in a teaching, positive way.

do you know . . . .

how to love . . . . ?

children

Children are such a unique blend of choice. It takes the choice of two people, to begin with, to even conceive a child … (and some people do not even comprehend the reality of their actions, at that moment, could possibly end up with the result of a child …). And, that "choice" lasts a lifetime!

A child has no choice to be born, or what circumstances they will be born into. It only takes a very short time, though, before this "new person" starts making "choices", whether they realize or not … based on their environment and interaction with life, and before long, they are young "individuals", with minds of their own. It does not take long before they are thinking thoughts for themselves, and making some of their own choices. The end result, is a person who is no longer a child, making choices of their own. And whether they were taught, or not, makes a huge difference whether they end up being a responsible adult, or an adult actually being a child themselves, never being taught the basics, having children themselves … you can see which cycle we would rather change.

The complex responsibility of having a child amazes me! They say that a child develops the major part of their personality by the time they are five years old. The choices that their parents make during that time, in those first five years, is vital to how a child turns out. There are so many responsible, wonderful people, who become parents in this World. Then, there are those that do not appreciate the "gift", abuse it and the result often shows in the child. What children experience, growing up, often determines what they will become, as adults. Each and every child deserves to be loved, cared for, encouraged … to be the "best" that they can be. Unfortunately, not every child gets what they deserve.

One of my goals, by writing this book, is to inspire all of us, to think before we act! To realize that we have a CHOICE of how we live our life. That "pause" and the conscious effort to be positive in the choices we make. This can make a difference in a child's life, (and in our own life). If we are always yelling at our children, do you think they get a positive feeling from that? I am convinced that input makes a huge difference in the outcome. All of us are people, first, and then parents. One element involving taking care of ourselves, so that we can take care of someone else … our children. Another element is knowledge … stepping back and being "rational" with children, as well as in your thoughts. The overall theme of rationality changed my life, because it changed my perspective. We will not always be perfect, and yet, realizing how important our reactions to our children actually are, will hopefully make you think, prior to negative reactions. Also, realizing that children are sometimes doing what they are, screaming … for example, there are other feelings behind their actions that they are too young to voice, causing frustration. If a parent yells back, what do you think that child thinks? If they could solve the "problem" differently, and voice it, they would. It is a difference in a parent's thinking that can make the difference between a teaching moment or meltdown.

Children look up to us, and learn from us … whether we are acting like we want them to end up, or acting like children, ourselves. If we are not aware of this, we may not stop to realize that every action and reaction is being watched, absorbed, and processed by our child. Before a child is five years old, they have basically formulated the overall "theme" of the personality … their actions and reactions. Many adults react to children like, "oh, go play … I'm busy …", and how is a child supposed to learn anything except, "I must not be very important". Hopefully, reacting to what you are reading, can have a positive impact on the interaction with your children. Teaching them, caring about how they perceive what is happening, loving their little spirits developing, based on what you are saying.

The wonder of it all, leaves me thankful for the opportunity that I had to be a Mother. My children are making exceptional choices, based on what I taught them . . . making them my "walking rewards". Their progress with life, their direction being taken and their choices along the way have been positive, productive and I could not ask for more … and this "theory" of mine, to teach power of choice with rational thinking, from a very early age, certainly was successful for me. In my opinion, the key to success is the "teaching" part, the knowledge but also the interaction in the learning process … the more we teach our children, the more diversified they will become.

To teach our children that they have choices about how they live their lives. It is not just "automatic", and life does not have to "have control over you", the opposite is true. To realize that we can pause, moment by moment … mentally monitor to make sure we are "on track", and THEN react … what a good "tool", moving forward. Our past does not equal our future, and even if you made mistakes yesterday, it does not mean that you cannot choose to make different choices tomorrow. The power in that message, for ourselves, as well as our children, is a powerful message to be taught. Over time, if practiced, it will begin to have a self-nurturing affect on the societies of the World. It is a Universal message … to be taught universally … and it can have a huge impact in generations to come.

The power of knowledge, in parents learning HOW to parent … just because you have a child does not automatically teach you what you need to know. You may feel isolated or unsure, and knowing that we have a new freedom to make positive choices … maybe a parenting class, or reaching out to a family or friend, asking for help … all of the "basics" that anyone who has had a child feels from time to time. A theme is "being OK with yourself", "getting to know yourself", "being more sure of yourself" … knowing that you have more than one choice, just that, in itself, may be an extremely powerful message for some people, who never realized that before.

Sometimes we are "our own worst enemy", with negativity dwelling in our thoughts and mind. What message does that send to our children? If you feel that way, I encourage you to reach out for help. And, realize that there is always potential for change, depending on choice ... your choices over a period of time may have developed a rut? Been there, done that! Never feel alone, there is always someone who can relate to what you are going through, especially as a Parent. This book wants to encourage wellness for everyone ... I have gone through my own set of circumstances because of my choices, AND I UNDERSTAND. Children, and life in general ... relationships, and family, work and responsibilities ... life in general has challenges, no matter what. It is not what happens, that matters. It is "how you react".

I feel extremely blessed with the Children with whom God gave to me. He knew that I needed special children who would not cause a lot of problem, we had a lot of fun. My relationship with their Father was an ongoing challenge, for me, being a very soft spirit married to a First Sergeant, prior to the knowledge that I am sharing in this book, caused its' challenges, at times, for all of us. Without the opposite personalities we had, though, our children would have turned out much differently, I am convinced. My parenting partner had many different approaches, as a First Sergeant, and I was the soft, emotional one ... teaching them the basic elements of right and wrong with caring and compassion ... the unique blend that both of my children have, now, is exceptional ... they both contribute a lot, in their own unique ways. I am very proud of them both, and my daughter-in-law.

One thing, as a Parent, you can hope that you do well.....in instilling values and beliefs into your children, and that you will feel "right" with their choices, for spouses. Not your choice, it is theirs . . . yet, you have to accept and live with and love them, as your children do. I feel so fortunate that my Son's choice, for his Wife . . . I could not have done better myself, which is a very nice way to feel! They have a beautiful daughter, and a son a month away from being born, two more beautiful examples of genuine love between two people ... it is evident in everything that they do. For one thing, he does not want to interact with his wife, the way his Father did with his Mother . . . the first sergeant in him often brought out a stern side. Also, he is a lot like his Father, in that he is an exceptional Soldier, provider and Father to his Children. Everything a Mother, as she is going through the day by day details of teaching their child . . . an end result for both of my Children beyond my dreams!

One challenge for a Mother is watching a child go to War. I cannot even comprehend illness or death, God knows that I am not that strong! War for over three and a half years, three different tours, knowing that he was separated from his Wife, and they were both stationed in Germany for seven years. Thankfully, he came home ... we feel blessed, and he is forever injured from what he saw and had to live through. Any Mother or Father of a Soldier ... they KNOW that "special place" in their heart, tucked away for their loved one . . .I just had to mention, with great pride and thankfulness, my "baby boy" grew up to go to war . . . that, in itself, is an amazing concept!

My daughter, on the other-hand, she is such a unique blend of my husband and I. Her perspective of what we went through, as a family, is different ...she was only two when we moved to Germany, for example ... she feels like she missed out. From the time she was born, though, she has been independent. She also has known what she wanted, from the time she was four years old. We would talk through her thoughts and dreams, every day ... she was very definite, and I believed that she could do it! Guess what? Twenty-one years later, it is exactly what she is doing! And I could not be more proud . . . I knew the entire time that there was no question about it. She directed herself, throughout her life ... always pushing ahead, determined, graduated early and off to L.A. ..at age eighteen, downtown L. A. for her or war for my son ... about the same, in my heart!

Two successful children, one of them happily married with children, and one pursuing her dreams, what a reward in life. It did not "just happen", though, and I did not just "send my kids out to play". I was constantly teaching, involving them with good activities, and then keeping up with that ... no matter what, my children came first. I have no regrets ... only positive, like an investment of time ... now it is coming back to me tenfold ... amazing, which makes me a very happy person.

How your children develop, and how they turn out, largely has to do with how you interact with them, each and every day, moment by moment ... the choices you make, as the adult, has an impact in your child, whether you realize, or not. They absorb more than you may realize, and I am convinced that thinking of children as "little people", is the best approach. It is one of my goals, in writing this, to enlighten and enhance you, as you read, maybe seeing a bit of yourself in what I say, or getting an idea of how you could think or do something differently? When I was introduced to a lot of this thinking, I had never heard of it before ... and I had been thinking and reacting much differently, in many ways.

As time goes on, I cannot even comprehend the way I used to be. But ... "you don't know, if you don't know" . . . that, is a BIG reason I am writing this. To share with anyone else who may have something in common with what I am saying ... sharing information ... a good thing ...

rational thinking .....

will ....

change your life........

what is best ....

for ....

your children ....

do you ....

want change? ....

education

When I think back on my education, it was basic and good, very special to me, in many ways. I will say, though, that there was a lot about life, looking back, that I wish would have been part of the educational process ... they left the basics such as balancing a checkbook, how to invest, how to write a resume, how to budget money, how to cook, the importance of good nutrition, many basics of life. I am sure that a lot was introduced, and I may have been goofing around, not listening. Learning is a "process", which needs to be fun and good, and ongoing "nourishing" way to spend time, and the interaction while being taught.

The main elements of education can be enhanced with the knowledge of rational thinking, and the power of choice. If those two concepts are introduced, at every level, it would only enhance the entire process, and help people change their perspective in their approach to life. The more exposure to different things, the better, in my opinion. My children and I have had a lot of exposure, Worldwide, from Germany, to the East coast, to the Pacific Northwest. My Son was born in Hawaii and his first four years were spent at the beach. My daughter spent her first birthday at the Smithsonian in Washington D.C., asleep on my shoulder. She crawled around castles in Germany her first four years, and we had fun exploring everywhere we went.

In my opinion, the best education, is experience. I would integrate education, on the basic traditional sense is necessary, to a point. But the thought process behind the idea that time only happens once. Is an hour of geometry more important? Or, learning to budget money?, for example. I would just ask the School districts in each State to examine the overall emphasis on tests, etc, and focus more on rational thinking, the power of choice, and all that goes along with that. I intend to write a children's version of "Choices", to relate the concept at a more elementary, simple way. Ways to practice with their thoughts, to make it creative and fun, and develop the potential we all have, that we do not even approach discovering. New frontiers of education, with rational thinking as a theme, can start changing the overall destruction and negativity of everyone's thought process...any positive influence is better than what the current reality actually is.

One reason that I want to discuss and change education, in some ways, is the urgent need to save our children from so much that they have to experience at home. There are very many loving, wonderful families in this World. There are probably as many, or more, of the opposite. How are we to know? To single out a child and say, "is it not very good at home"? That just cannot happen, for many reasons. And yet, how can we expect a child to succeed, if they are subjected to adverse conditions at home. "If we only knew?" ... "We probably don't want to?" ... the poor children, and what some have to live with? Oh my gosh, we, as a society ... (if we want any chance of future healing, for the World), we need to heal our children, and start providing for them. They did not ask to come into this World under adverse conditions. I only know that if we introduce rational thinking, and the power of choice, and many other basic concepts ... for each of our Children, to teach them .... they will treat us well ...

Our Nation, the United State of America, is a great nation and leader in the World. There are many nations, though, that lead the United States, in many ways. I would think that this new administration would be extremely intelligent, if they looked closely to what I am saying about "rational thinking" involved in education. The theme of this forward thought could enhance, to say the least, and revolutionize if we really stand back and look at all of the wasted ways this World functions! It was all started in the education of our children, if we are going to stand back and look at it all!

don't judge ....

unless ....

you are walking ....

In their shoes ....

a smarter, forward thinking . . .

trend ...

for ...

all

* * * * * * * * * * * * * * * *

rational thinking

frustration

Frustration is a choice. It is not because of the circumstances, there is the choice that you make of how to feel, about the circumstances. We all have the option to change what frustrates us ... "doing it", is a different matter. It is an emotional response, sometimes well practiced, which excels with no food and no sleep, or some food allergies, or lack of self learning about how to deal with the emotion differently. Just as with anything, there is more than one option, (choice), and depending on the choice, we determine the result. You can sit back and feel frustrated, or you can decide to feel differently.

There are some things that we cannot change . . . what we CAN do, though, is to change our thoughts, and our approach because of those thoughts. It takes practice, if you are a person that gets frustrated about something in Bosnia, for example. You are "setting yourself up", for negative feelings.

Only YOU can decide how you feel and how you react. If you allow yourself to get frustrated, about things you have no control over, you have the option not to do that, with the understanding of rational thinking. This has been difficult to write, because it "frustrates" me, when people allow themselves to get frustrated ... I am the opposite. Negative thoughts and feelings create frustration ... it is a negative way to feel ... and I do everything I can do, to feel good, no matter what!

Life is difficult enough, as it is. I have learned, over time, how to manage my time and my thought processes, to create a peaceful and calm "theme". Staying busy, keeping a positive attitude, monitoring my thoughts and what I allow into my life ... I rarely encounter a reason for frustration. There will always be obstacles ... the more we prepare, and know that it is a normal part of life, it is easier to roll along, hoping that your love is consistent, and you have a network of support system to back you up. I am not sure what I would do without my wonderful Mother, without her, I am not sure what I would do. I would "figure it out", I am sure ... but she helps me, in so many ways ... and only hope that I can return to her, at least a portion that she has given to me. Her consistent love is one exceptional way that I avoid frustration ... I leave it at the door, and "talk to Mom".

it is ....

what it is ....

and,

why am I thinking that?

failure

Is failure the opposite of success? Not necessarily. To me, failure is non-existent. There is no such thing as "failure"! To many people, it is how they live … thinking that they are a failure. In my opinion, it is all in what you CHOOSE to think about, and how. If you think you are a failure, chances are … that is what you will have a tendency to manifest. "You are what you think", is what they say. I believe that they are right. You do not have to be a failure, if you decide to make that choice, it is up to you … the things you think and the actions you take make all of the difference.

Society has "created" this label, along with it's definition of "success". If you just go along with believing what people tell you, then it can create huge problems for you, affecting your self- esteem and having a tendency to "paralyze" your actions. Negativity has it's way with everything, if you let it. That is one reason why I wanted to write this book, to remind you that it does not have to be that way. It makes such a difference … your perception, your belief about something, and "what you tell yourself". The basic elements of this book … the ongoing theme of rational thinking, and the power within yourself of how you CHOOSE to perceive life for yourself. You have the power of choice, of whether you let "society", (or anyone or anything else), influence how you think about yourself or the exceptional uniqueness you offer. Whether you take your own power to decide for yourself, to control your own thoughts and become the person of your choice. Or whether you give your power away, and succumb to the opinions of others? Why would you give your power away? That, in my opinion, is one definition of failure … (which I have also experienced) … to be so busy beating yourself up, because you do not fit into the definition that your family and/or our society has decided for you? Why would that happen?

Why would people think that THEY could decide what is best for us? Especially, if they are not walking in our shoes. This overall concept is very touching, for me, I have experienced this empty feeling of "not being right", sometimes, with the people who normally would be the most accepting. WRONG. Sometimes, the people you would think would be the most helpful, will become the most difficult to "please". And, if you only know that concept … if you have been taught to give up your own value on behalf of others … a "soft spirit" has a difficult time in life, because pleasing others does not always feel comfortable with your own heart. If you start in the direction that others think would be best for you, it is easy to be left feeling empty and confused . . . which sometimes can lead you to turn to chemicals such as drugs or alcohol, which sometimes leads to turning to people you might not normally associate with, just to "fit in" with someone, not feeling you are accepted by the "real" people in your life. It can become a downward spiral, with a lot of negativity … very difficult to escape from, and sometimes, is a deep hole of "failure" you cannot even realize is happening, until it already has.

As throughout this book, it is easy for me to relate to many different elements in this book, and the feeling of "failure" is one of them, and very difficult, no matter who you are. You can be homeless, or extremely wealthy, monetarily, and still feel like a failure from within. A big contributing factor is how your parents feel about what you are doing. Your family, and their opinions, need to keep to themselves … "if they do not have something nice to say", their opinions are their own. Everyone has one, it just does not need to be the same as your opinion of yourself. It has taken a lot of strength, inner-analysis, counseling, and living … to find peace with how my family feels about me. My Mother, bless her heart, she means well, has helped me beyond, and has been disappointed by my actions many, many times … so actually, she has a "right" to her opinion. Yet, if she only knew how much her opinion affects me.

Although I have tried some ventures and failed financially, which many people experience, it does not make me a "failure". It is very difficult to separate yourself, and your self-esteem, to pick yourself up and feel any kind of "normal" again, after the failure of a business, for example, or a marriage or any kind of failure. It takes time to heal, as in any loss, and it takes a huge commitment to yourself … to take the time, especially during this time, to "practice" rational thinking. It may seem like a waste of time? The exact opposite is true. During your worst times, is when you need rational thinking and your power of choice the most. To DEC IDE that you are "OK the way you are, and not equal to your failure". Ongoing self-talk can make or break your spirit, following a difficult business venture or disappointment?"

One thing that I had to learn, as I went along practicing rational thinking and the power of choice. It took awhile to give myself permission, to separate myself from what everyone else thought.

It was like a new freedom, and it took awhile to also adapt to the self discipline, when I could no longer blame anyone else, and that I had to take responsibility for myself, good and bad. It is a "new" way to live, to have the ability to "decide" whether to feel good or not. When you realize that you "have the controls", not your outside influence that you have allowed to control you for so long. Although most of us let go of others' opinions as we go through the trials of being a teenager, some of us do not realize this choice of freedom of thought until we have long been adults, having "gone along" with others and their opinions of our lives for a long time. It may be a "lightbulb moment" as you are reading this …

Failure may be an accumulation of wrong choices over a very long time. It may be a label a teacher or parent puts on you from a very early age. If you think about it, you may even be doing this to someone else, thinking that your judgment knows more about their choices than they know about themselves. Who gives you that right? Even though I am a Mother of two, and Mother-in-Law of one, thankfully for the training I have had, I realize that I absolutely do not have the right to think that I know what my children should do with their lives. And luckily, by teaching them independence the way I did, they have been making exceptional choices along the way. My daughter, I do my best to "shelter" her from a lot of the mistakes that I made along the way. I counselor her, and yet do my best to help her stand back and think rationally for herself, and to realize her own power of choice. She gets tired of my "theme", at times, and yet she knows that I have a lot to say, most of the time.

Having made many "mistakes" along the way, it brings up the topic of regret. Do I regret some of what I have done? Yes, some of my choices have been horrible, at times I have been my own worst enemy. At times, I have let others lead and I have followed … at one point being conned by someone who abused my vulnerability and my financial situation, at the time. Then, when the money was gone … so was he! And it even took awhile to realize, then admit that I could be so "stupid", that I even allowed this to happen to myself. And sometimes, with chemical imbalance involved … choices and situations get distorted … becoming something much different that you thought it was for yourself, then a pattern very difficult to get away from. If I had not experienced that particular situation, it would be much easier for me to sit back and judge someone else, for exactly the same behavior. Having gone through it, at a very vulnerable time I went through, it makes me much more compassionate for those who find themselves in that similar situation. And, it made me stand back and re-evaluate family and friends, saying that they care, when their judgment "cuts like a knife". A "thick skin", is one thing that I developed during this time. And a huge lesson in forgiveness … forgiveness of myself, and everyone who misunderstood what I lived through.

Bouncing back from "failure" is very difficult, if you do not have the realization of the power of choice. When you think that you are a victim of circumstances, when you think that life "did this to you", and when you feel powerless over how to change your circumstances ... of course you feel stuck! Also, a mistake that I have made in the past, is to think that I need to change everything all at the same time. What finally made a difference, for me, is to realize that I had the power to make changes for myself, one small step at a time ... to keep on taking a "baby step", ongoing, being patient ... yet pushing, especially when I did not think that I could do it. Self-talk ... instead of beating myself up for the mistakes, to SEVER the PAST, start fresh with a clean slate, (an extremely powerful part of a better future), and I realized that getting overwhelmed about the entire situation did not help. To step back, and take it just a little bit at a time, it made the difference, for me.

everyone ...

has a story ....

sever the past ....

make the choice ....

change your future ....

the process of change

You can go from being that "couch potato", to being ambitious ... one step at a time. You can do anything that you decide to do ... the power of choice, with rational thinking, can change your life. Not overnight, and not without a lot of effort and conscious choice. It can happen, though, and I am living proof. My life is completely different than it was, and although being judged for what I am NOT doing, I am very proud of myself. You can accomplish the same personal satisfaction, with a shift of thinking. If you just start realizing that you DO have the power of choice in your life!

Many of you reading this book, may have a success story. Many of you may be like me, who struggled along, learning as I went. Nothing was handed to me, except the strongest base full of love and support that a person could ever dream of. My problem in life, as I approached it? That I was loved and sheltered too much, if you can believe that. The fact that I had never experienced any adversity ... it took awhile to even realize how to react when it was happening to me ... I did not even realize, at first, and my body just started "hurting to breathe", until I sat down and talked it through to discover what I had been stuffing, trying to make it be good for myself, even though it was not. As time went on, I had to toughen up, and "get real", with how life is, for most. Not the secluded, peaceful, wonderful life created by my parents. If you come from that background, like I did, it is an extra blessing to have that base. It just takes adjustment, as you progress through life.

You may say to yourself, "I do not even know how to think rationally, what do I do"? I felt the same way, even after practicing in classes for two years. It is a process … it takes a lot of practice, in an ongoing way, to be patient and understanding with yourself because you are learning something new, like a baby. As time goes on, you start feeling the "theme", with your power of choice based on your new rational thoughts. It does not happen overnight, keep remembering that it is a process. And as you start feeling and seeing results with your own choices, it will make you want to start sharing this new knowledge with your important people in your life, especially your children. You will start recognizing, in others, the irrational thoughts and actions, and some of what you cannot control will become more in perspective. It is like a new awakening, a positive light, a lightness with peace and calm within you. If you fast forward, you can become surprised, even with your own progress … when you realize the power within you to take control of your own thoughts and actions, it will bring a new enlightenment to yourself.

Then, if you feel that new, positive, special feeling of "not being so bad after all", it starts the new process of automatically spreading a positive light, everywhere you go, and with everything you do. Just like my son, who went to a class where they reminded him that it was a good thing to express how he felt. This book, I hope, will spread a message. It is extremely good for you to be "who you are", and bringing the best to the surface. Eliminating the negativity, that life has built up in you, can be an exceptional gift for yourself and the World.

Anyone who is reading this book, who feels like a failure, broken, a waste? I urge you to reach out and get help. And one of the first things to examine, as you move through your choices, is to get tested for thyroid imbalance, and other imbalance, in your system. It is amazing how just one slight imbalance, in our physical systems, can bring many different systems out of balance. Irritability, feeling stress, alcohol imbalance, nicotine which affects the "roller coaster" of personality … when part of you is broken, it causes a ripple effect. If any of this sounds like anything that could be affecting you and your family, I urge you to reach out for help!

Fear of failure can play a very important part in the process of moving forward. Although it may only be a word, "failure", it also has a huge stigma that goes along with it. For someone to begin in the depths of "failure", or to find themselves falling into that "pit" along the way, it is a very difficult way to experience life. At times, even coming from a very nice place, it felt like I would always be in that "ditch", (when I found myself there). To know, now, what it took to get here … it only makes me want to share more with others. "If I can do it, ANYONE can do it!" Maybe you have heard it before… now, you can believe it. With these tools for life, involving the Power of Choice, and Rational Thinking … and making a decision for yourself to push forward, anything is possible.

People have a tendency to "feel like a failure", if they do not "feel successful". And, so often, all of this applies to the financial part of their life. When we can gain another perspective, realizing that what we tell ourselves, makes such a big difference in the results. For one thing, there are so many ways that we can be "successful", without having much money. And many successful, rich people, are completely broken. How we perceive ourselves, that is our own responsibility. We owe it to ourselves to find out what works best for ourselves, and if we do not take care of ourselves, no one else will.

If, for example, you read these words … then you make the decision to change. That would be a blessing, don't you think? Whatever it takes, if you do not like something about yourself. It took a lot of pain, before I discovered these special ways to relate to myself. I am continually reminding myself, after nine years of knowing about these freeing concepts. I still have to tell myself that I do not have to get emotionally attached to what something that someone might say, in passing. Knowing how I used to be, and knowing how to separate myself from who I was, now, it is the best gift that I give to myself, constantly. It is a constant calming affect that I feel, rather than any aggravation, based on past beliefs. Once a Mother, always a Mother. And, when I take the time to talk to myself, reminding myself that I feel that way, but that is okay … it makes me want to take a deep breath, and react (both internally and in reaction), with love, kindness, and the thought that no bad intention can ever affect who I am.

Sometimes, we read into something, that was not even there. In this process of change, that new knowledge will provide for you, a process of wanting to react differently, because you will start thinking differently, which will help you focus more upon yourself and your own needs. Then, once you heal, you will want to share with others, less fortunate, who need help ... in any way you can share it. Once someone starts feeling better, especially if they have not been doing so well, and when they start finding ways to tell themselves that they have the power of change ... it becomes contagious. Thankfully, there are the people who find themselves with success, already. They share as much as they possibly can, which is "how they roll". If we can spread the word to become our own powerful, positive advocates ... doing what we love to do, and sharing it with others, the positive will pay forward, ending hunger, and helping those who need it the most. This book, for example, is my way of giving to the World. Writing has been my passion for a very long time, I wrote portions of this book over twenty years ago. Now, though, is the time to share this with you, because looking back, I had not even been introduced to the Power of Choice, based on Rational Thought.

If we can begin to heal ourselves, one step at a time, using the concept involving rational thinking, and if we can accept the fact that we are our own best advocate. If we can start thinking that "yes, we can" .... if our thought processes can be positive ... we will change!

A child does not start out knowing whether he/she is important ... they learn their "place in life", from their parents. If they do not get the positive information that they need, they automatically start thinking negatively ... "I must be the reason why my parents fight", for example. It is amazing that people grow up "functioning", as well as they do. At times, the message our children get in no way supports their inner spirit or their unique gifts they have inside of them to offer this World.

If parents nurture, promote positive thinking, express their feeling, teach their children right from wrong, then having their actions be good examples of what real life is all about. Each and every child is so uniquely unique! What they perceive? How they perceive it? What they are taught? A clean slate becomes very complex, in a very short period of time.

After reading this information, hopefully it will give you pause, to step back and take a look at how you may be reacting to your own children? Do you continuously keep saying, "just a minute, Daddy is busy looking at his cell phone screen", for example. Or do they get from him, "sure, Honey, I would love to spend time with you, because I have to be away at work so much …" I cherish every moment I spend with you, Child of Mine, and I am in awe of who you are and want to be part of who you become"! Just an example. How often, recently, as I am driving along and see a bus stop, instead of parents talking to their children or each other … every adult has their head in their cell phones. It is another reason for this book … I resist technology, and suffer in ways because of it. Thankfully, my Children understand and love me, and help me. Without them, especially when my Daughter-in-Law went totally out of her way, to help me limp through technological requirements I had for one job. Without her help, it would have jeopardized my job. She taught me a little at a time, so that I did not get overwhelmed … eventually, we made it to the next step. It is good to ask for help, if there is no other way you can figure it out. That is part of the uniqueness of each of us, having different "gifts", to give to each other.

Changing is not easy, and even having new thoughts and new ways to approach your life, it will be an ongoing challenge. So if you expect anything except perfect, and flexibility that everything is going to be okay, it will make it much easier to change. Many times, we set up our expectations … (which, I believe it is good to envision a plan). And yet, we need to always have a "winning" Plan B, Plan C and Plan D. If we always live with an attitude of flexibility, then nothing will be able to confront us with paralyzing results. We set ourselves up for disappointment, at times, when we "decide" what would be best … then if life dishes us another set of circumstances, for whatever reason, we also "decide" to make a "choice" to react with negative energy, rather than having a perspective, automatically reacting in a positive way, one way or another.

Until you change your thought processes to the "positive side of life", if you are not there now, and until you realize that you are your own "Captain of your Plane", soaring through life with the power within you to make unbelievable choices for yourself. Rational thinking is a powerful way of being able to achieve great potential, with ongoing practice and learning. There is already a division around the World, between those who want Peace, and those who want War. Now, knowing that there is potential for Peace for each and every human being on Earth, the key is getting knowledge to the right Leaders of the World, that decisions made with Rational Thinking, have much more potential for success and peace for everyone!

The process of change is complex. It involves letting go of old ways, to make way for new ways … new patterns, new thinking, new decisions and choices. All of this can take place, it really can, if you make that choice. Or, it can happen any way that makes a difference for you. Each of us have different "triggers" of what "works for us". Anything as major as stopping an addictive habit, to a gnawing small habit, anything is possible, if you believe it to be so. We all started the same way, as human beings, we started as very tiny, helpless individual little people, who needed help with everything...even the most powerful person (or so they think), needed help as an infant. Persecution, with ongoing beliefs... bullying with ongoing beliefs … so it goes, in some parts of the World. If we can start to educate EVERYONE, that it is a birth right to have the power of choice … common thinking and rational living would change this World, if the people begin to think this is true. It is, what it is.

conclusion

Thank you for taking the time to read this book. It means that you, at least, cared enough about yourself, to absorb what was said. It will be a test of time, whether you start noticing a difference in the way you think, and whether it changes anything about how you approach your life. Anything from being a subtle change, to making a huge connection ...any results in a positive direction, will be the result hoped for. There seems to be so much negativity, even for me ... who filters in every way what I allow into my life. "Garbage in, Garbage out ...", it is an overall theme, for my life. What I allow into my life must enhance it. And all of the mystery, murder, court, gossip, tragedy, etc, all of the negative, in every way, is a "waste of my time". "I only have so much of it .... time ..."

If people would only stop to realize, that every second, of every day, of every year ... is a choice! With education, rational thinking and determination, those choices can be productive and good. With misinformation, past negative results to draw upon (rather than severing the past and starting fresh), by allowing others' beliefs to influence us, even if that is not how we feel ... to be in a circumstance or situation not authentic to who we really are ... does any of this sound familiar? The "habit of negativity", it has a way of deteriorating the quality of life, in one way or another ... and some people look at a negative way of life as the only way of life. Each of us has a choice, and if that is their choice? So be it. I, personally, cannot comprehend how anyone can want such negative energy as part of their lives? I am convinced, though, that knowledge is power. Rational thinking promotes action that makes sense, and eliminates any ways to spend time that do not!

"sever the past" ... "move forward" ... "with a smile on your face"

care about others

and

live positively and rationally

it will

change the world

change – the process

When you make the CHOICE, that there is a "new you", inside of you … it will give you an opportunity to create an entirely new life. You may be at a place in your life, where you like a lot of how you are. You may only need to make a few changes, from your perspective, (prior to knowing about rational thinking and the power within you to make choices that are good for YOU). You may be a criminal, sitting in jail … wondering, "how did I end up here"? You may want only minor changes, you may want an entirely new life! Change is never easy. I do know, though, from personal experience, that it is possible, with forward motion and determination.

The main element of change is "choice". You have the choice to feel good or bad. You have the choice to be positive or negative. You have the choice to take action, or just sit there. And if you are a person sitting in jail, you can either educate yourself, or not. When you make the choice that there is a "new you", inside of you …you can either take action, or not. Sometimes it takes coaching from yourself, or others … but everyone on the Earth has potential, in one way or another. When you realize that every single moment involves choice, then you start looking at your thoughts in a different way … just because you have been a certain way, does not mean that you have to continue to be that way. Did you know that? I didn't, for a very long time. You have the power to change, if you decide to … you just need to know that you have that "power", then believe it, then take action in making choices that change your results.

You have to WANT to change. It does not just happen. You cannot keep blaming every other person for your problems, or your past, or your ....nothing makes any difference, if you sever it, take responsibility for yourself and your own actions, and begin in a new, exciting way forward. Being thankful, is always a good theme. Planning, having vision of your direction, knowing that you have the power to make new choices, and believing in yourself, maybe for the first time in your life ... it can be very enlightening and life changing. Some people never realized, before, that they had any control over what happens to them. Any type of suppression, taking choices away from any individual, is negative and wrong, in my opinion. It possibly is beyond my capacity, at this point. Although, this information is positive, good, and powerful ... the future impact is yet to be known...

It is up to YOU. Each of us has a responsibility to each other, to take care of each other, and to care when others are hurting themselves or others. It is a very small World, unique, overwhelming and unexplainable . . . . "it is, what it is ..." That applies to everything, to accept what is, and to see what needs to improve. That is an ongoing theme ... over time ... hoping that the "good guys win"! It seems like a helpless place, to be an innocent, vulnerable individual in this World ... amongst all of the irrational thinking in the World, amongst each other. Why? Somehow, some of these beliefs and feelings started, somewhere and somehow ... people are losing their lives because of it? When you learn to think rationally, FACTS like this will make you cringe!

When you, as an individual, start to realize that you can go from helpless to powerful, just with a change in your attitude. And by practicing that attitude, and teaching that overall concept to your children, it can have an impact in changing the World ... maybe not overnight, but eventually, if enough people start realizing the difference between the way it is now, and the potential for this World with rational thinking and cooperation ... think if all of the Nations could come together, stop the fighting ... and start helping each other ... the World would start to heal itself ...

When you remember that the main element of change ... is "choice", it has a completely different dimension, because new options surface, when you start believing in that potential. The direction we focus on, positive or negative, is the direction that our life will go. It is up to us to direct ourselves . . . why do they not tell us, and teach us this, in the first place? I was a mature adult when I was introduced to a lot of this information. I would urge the active people involved in developing the direction of our education ... around the World, having a theme of rational thinking, forward motion, and "new thinking", involving the power of choice, within each of us, and not really talked about. With this new information also comes responsibility, to direct those choices with intelligence, positivity, and a way of blending with others' choices to help others.

"You don't know, if you don't know", and I didn't, for a very long time. Then, after I learned a lot of what I share with you, it took quite a long time to adopt it as my version of the way I wanted to spend my life. I waivered, for years, giving my power away to others, not realizing that I could "decide" to feel better. I was a victim of circumstances, that hurt my feelings to this day, and there is nothing that I can do to change that. My counselor and I questioned, from every direction, how to let go of that pain. Some things, they will never be the same!

One way, sometimes, if you do not like some things about yourself? Start making some subtle changes in your appearance, your style ... maybe, what you eat, and where? Are there any patterns that would be quite easy to change, that would remind you of the internal changes you want to make, such as ... thinking more rationally and realizing that you have the power inside of you to take control of the choices you make! Sometimes, a new hair style and/or color, a new outfit, maybe a new ring sparkling at you to remind you of "the new you"? (When I say something like that, then think of a global audience reading this book, it almost sounds silly thinking of the girl walking a mile to get water for her family, when I mention buying a new ring). My limited exposure, please forgive me, if I am completely ignorant to many societies and cultures in this World, each of us could learn a lot from each other.

Of course, I am not saying that this is necessary. And each of you knows what you can do to remind yourself of new change, until it becomes a new normal for you. At first, the "step by step" process of rational thinking can seem cumbersome. I remember sitting in class, going around … one by one … taking a thought and dissecting it into whether it was rational, or not, and why. My counselors were exceptional, gifts from God, for me … I will never forget them, carefree, loving, calm, compassionate, loving ways. I could go on and on. Today, I can totally relate to their inner peace, their casual, special way to be … being able to not be emotionally involved in what is happening … anything they did not have control of, they let go of. I, now, can think and flow freely with life, living moment by moment, making choices that are good for me, regardless of anyone else's "vote". Only I know what is best for me … no one else. Difficult to remember that, at times.

It is all an ongoing process, you never really just know … you hope that, over time, you gain consistence with knowledge of rational thinking always involved in every decision and choice. Not always, though … you can think that you "have it", then … lack of sleep? Too much traffic? From out of nowhere, at times, no matter how long you have been living with rational thinking, you can become the most irrational individual on the planet! As long as you are humble, you know that every person goes through difficult, uncomfortable times … here and there … sometimes irrational thought …

The "changing process" takes concentration, determination, effort … it does not just happen. I am here telling you, though, and had it not been for my wonderful, caring counselors … I dedicate a lot of this to them, who taught me how to think differently, and the fact that it was even possible. I will always have a very special place in my heart for my "teachers", along the way …my Mother included! Without them, I am not sure where I would be....definitely not as well as I am, which has definitely been a "process".

First of all, it takes the decision that you want to change... not everyone thinks that they need to. Maybe not? This is only one perspective. It is my opinion … my point of view on how you can enhance the life you already have. Or, if you choose to, you can completely change your life. It is all up to you.

There are some steps that I used to change some major things, both stopping drinking and smoking cigarettes happened because at X-rays … of my own body, at different times. For some reason, in both instances, that was enough to see my own body deteriorating because of my choices, and it was easy for me to make the decision to stop, after seeing those X-rays … I never looked back.

A decision, a change in your habits and patterns, reminding yourself, gently, from time to time … that you have a new way to be, not wanting the old anymore … the old habits were gone! I introduced to myself, for stopping smoking cigarettes, for example … I call it "replacement therapy", thinking rationally about the situation. I analyzed it, realizing that it involves my mouth, the sensation of the hand to mouth "attention". Also, breathing was an important part, for me. So I adopted a special pen, my quit smoking pen. And I always kept close by, a new, special fruity mint … it took the place of needing to do something having to do with hands, mouth, and the "ritual". For me, it worked quite easily, even though I continued to do exactly the same things, in the same environment, with smokers. No irritability, no side affects, no chemical help … mints and a pen. Each of us has the power of choice, if we make that decision. If I can do it? You for sure can do anything you set your mind to, in a thoughtful, determined way … working WITH yourself, and the way you know that you are. It is possible, anything is, if you believe that you can do it, change some of your actions and reactions, and "just do it".

Any change can be accomplished, using the same process … (I used that as an example because everyone knows of its' difficulty). Any change can be difficult, easy, anything inbetween … depending on what works for you. Decide on the change, interrupt the old habits, develop some new patterns that work for you, replacing the old with something new that you enjoy. Stay busy, use concentrated effort, at first … eventually the change will seem natural, if that is your choice. Not easy … it can be accomplished. Practice, patience with yourself, and commitment to change.

Sometimes, we need to accept "what is", and accept ourselves just the way we are for awhile, before we can move to the "next level", and adapt to a new way to be. This way of thinking is different, in some ways, and very real and normal in other ways … maybe some things that you already know, just being reminded helps. Others, like I was, had never realized how much power I was giving to others, and not making my own decisions, based on what was best for myself. Over time, imbalance happened, for me … it took a lot to get it all back in balance, but do not think it is not possible, because it is …. anything is possible, that you decide for yourself!

your choices.............

equal...........

who you are ....

think about it ......

Every person has their own set of circumstances. They have to approach change in their own way, in their own time. The main thing that I want to inspire, and make you feel is possible, is that you CAN change, if you want to. If you do not, at least by reading this, you gained a different perspective involving rational thinking, and a way to enhance the life that you already have developed. You can either let life control you, or you can realize that you can control your own life! Moment by moment, do you like the way you interact and relate to people, and your circumstances?

Do you really live your life to the fullest, or do you just "function"? Each and every one of us make hundreds of choices, on a daily basis ... an ongoing process, whether we realize or not. So many of our choices are based upon how we feel? What our priorities are? Often based on patterns and habits that have been in our lives for awhile, without even thinking about. So many of us are afraid of change, or have no depth to see that we need change? There are so many variables, and choices, that each of us make each and every day.

Sometimes, it is best to write down our direction, so that we have an idea of what steps we need to accomplish to get the results we want. Others, it is a difficult task, just to write ... formulating things in your mind can be just as sure, as long as you make the commitment to yourself. It can make a big difference, even to just make the choice to change. It does not mean that it will happen overnight, and you cannot just snap your fingers and have it happen. With an open mind and the right approach, though, anything is possible. If we started relaying that message to our children, more . . . over a period of time, we would raise more independent, satisfied, calm individuals that know themselves, and know what they want from life and how to get what they want.

You do not have to do anything, unless you want to. That is the special, positive, good part about becoming aware of this knowledge ... we all have the power within us, "to be, or not to be"? That is a very old question, and yet a good one. Do you want to sit back and let this life pass you by? Or do you want to start adapting some of what has been said in this book, and one step at a time, make a difference for ourselves, and therefore, make a difference in this World. This is my attempt, at accomplishing just that.

write down examples of:

what changes?

when? (be specific)

rational thinking – worksheets

examples of the old and new style ......

write down ....

how do you want to make different choices for yourself?

rational thinking – worksheets
potential?

write down your new
potential ....

more rational
thinking - worksheets

examples of the old vs. new Style

write down what changes ... when ... how you want to make different choices for yourself ...

more rational
thinking - worksheets

what is your potential?

the first step ......

is always .....

the biggest ....

you are special .....

start feeling that way ....

about the author

Born and raised in Washington State … she is a person who has learned about life, step by step, quietly developing her philosophy and beliefs. With a unique combination of "success and failure", with counseling by very loving, devoted people, who shared ways to negotiate through life.

Being a sensitive, caring individual … and marrying a First Sergeant in the United States Army, and having two beautiful children … (one in Hawaii and one in Virginia … plus a tour in Germany), they had their "adventures". It gave her a lot of insight into her authentic self … who she had become, a Mother, first and foremost … the most cherished gift, to her. And underlying, in her life, though … being an "author".

To finally realize her "dream/goal", of publishing this book … (first written over twenty years ago), a result from her heart. It will offer a sense of accomplishment … to devote time and energy to share her "version" … her authentic self.

More books will follow … the first step is always the BIGGEST … and the most rewarding gift to share …

did you ......

gain anything ....

by reading ....

this book....?

What did you gain ....?

future books planned

Hard Cover

Coffee Table Version

Calendar Version

"Her Story" ….. a novel

Choices … for Children

Choices … for Teens

Choices … for Seniors, and those Caring for Themselves

Choices … and Addiction

Choices … and Controlling Weight

Choices … the Wrong Ones

Choices … saying Good-bye for a Year and a Half

Printed in the United States
By Bookmasters